A CITY UPON A HILL

Speeches by Ronald Reagan

Before the Conservative

Political Action Conference

1974-1988

Edited by
James C. Roberts

ISBN 0-931727-07-3

A CITY UPON A HILL

Speeches by Ronald Reagan
Before the Conservative
Political Action Conference

1974–1988

A Joint Project of

The American Conservative Union
The American Studies Center
Human Events, Inc.

EDITED BY JAMES C. ROBERTS

The American Conservative Union is the nation's oldest conservative lobbying organization. Founded in 1964, the purpose of ACU was to establish a single group that could effectively communicate the goals and principles of conservatism. ACU's Statement of Principle makes clear their support of capitalism, opposition to communism and Soviet expansion, belief in the doctrine of original intent of the framers of the Constitution, confidence in traditional moral values, and commitment to a strong national defense.

Over the years, ACU has been on the cutting edge of major public policy battles. Opposing the Panama Canal giveaway, fighting to keep OSHA off the backs of small businesses, opposing the SALT treaties, supporting aid to freedom fighters in Marxist countries, promoting the confirmation of conservative Justices to the Supreme Court and supporting the near-term deployment of strategic defenses have been some of the more significant efforts of the American Conservative Union.

—The American Conservative Union

The American Studies Center is a non-profit tax-exempt foundation as designated by Section 501(c)(3) of the Internal Revenue Service code. The ASC is dedicated to traditional American values, limited government, a free economy, and a strong national defense. The foundation affirms its commitment to these principles through a wide-ranging program of conferences, publications and radio and television productions.

—The American Studies Center

The Declaration of Independence begins: "When in the course of *Human Events*...." In reporting the news HUMAN EVENTS is objective; it aims for accurate presentation of all the facts. But it is not impartial. It looks at events through eyes that are biased in favor of limited constitutional government, local self government, private enterprise and individual freedom. These principles represented the bias of the Founding Fathers. We think the same bias will preserve freedom in America.

—Human Events

Contents

Introduction

The Conservative Political Action Conference, held annually since 1974 in Washington, D.C., has become the most important yearly event for conservative activists around the nation.

CPAC, as the conference is known, is a successor to the old political action conferences sponsored by *Human Events*, the weekly conservative newspaper, in the 1960s. The first CPAC Conference, held in 1974, was organized at a time when conservatives were profoundly disillusioned with the policy drift of the Nixon administration, and demoralized by the scandal-induced resignation of Vice President Spiro Agnew and the unfolding Watergate tragedy.

To conservative leaders and activists alike it seemed as though the resurgent conservative movement which had displayed such vigor and purpose in the Goldwater effort of 1964 and the Nixon victory of 1968 was drifting and in danger of collapse.

In a series of meetings, conservative office holders and organization heads had concluded that a national conference was needed as a means of uniting the disparate elements of the movement and refocusing its political and policy goals.

Ronald Reagan, then in the last year of his second term as Governor of California, was the overwhelming choice to be principal speaker at the conference. The chairmen of the American Conservative Union and Young Americans for Freedom extended an invitation to him to speak, and it was accepted.

The first conference was set for January 1974 with the American Conservative Union and Young Americans for Freedom as principal co-sponsors working in cooperation with *Human Events* and *National Review*. A host of other conservative groups signed on as participating organizations.

I had reported aboard the American Conservative Union in early 1974 and recall plunging immediately into a series of

12-hour days as the small ACU and YAF staffs scrambled to cope with the flood of details inherent in a national conference of that scale.

The publicity for the conference trumpeted the announcement "Governor Reagan comes to Washington," and indeed he did—eventually to stay for eight years.

The CPAC conferences are linked inextricably with Ronald Reagan's long campaign for the Presidency and his eight years in the White House, and his speeches there reflect a unique relationship that he forged and maintained over the span of a decade and a half with the conservative movement in America.

The President was the featured speaker at every conference from 1974 to 1988 with the exceptions of 1976 and 1980, when he was campaigning in the Republican primary in New Hampshire. This book contains the texts of all these addresses except for the 1979 speech, which has been lost.

The 12 addresses reprinted here will be of interest to layman and historian alike, for what they say about Ronald Reagan, the man, the politician, and the President.

Of paramount importance—in my mind at least—is what the speeches say about Reagan as a man of ideas. Ronald Reagan has been underestimated for many reasons by many people— many of whom have ended up as vanquished foes.

One of the most egregious misrepresentations of Reagan, however, is that he is a shallow, poorly read man with a simplistic mindset informed by bromides, Hollywood myths and apocryphal stories culled from right wing journals.

The truth is much different. Ronald Reagan is, to be sure, a man "set in his ways." He has a political philosophy, belives in a body of principles and holds strong views about what the world is really like.

Yet his philosophy, principles and world view are informed by a life of wide-ranging experiences and by extensive reading.

Ronald Reagan is one of a small group of American presidents who cared about ideas, who had a vision of what America was all about and what it should become, and who entered the White House with a program to translate this vision into reality.

Ronald Reagan has the distinction of being one of the few

leaders of a political movement to be elected President, a feat he accomplished because of his political prowess, his oratorical skills and the compelling nature of his message.

History's assessment of the Reagan presidency is yet to be written, but whatever that is, it seems clear now that Ronald Reagan is one of the most remarkable leaders of our time.

These 12 speeches before the Conservative Political Action Conference, taken together, comprise a revealing political portrait of our 40th President.

JAMES C. ROBERTS
Washington, D.C.
September 8, 1989

I

'We Will Be As A City Upon a Hill...'

January 25, 1974

When Ronald Reagan addressed the first Conservative Political Action Conference on January 25, 1974, the conservative movement was in danger of disintegrating. The disappointment caused by many of Richard Nixon's foreign and domestic policy achievements was compounded by the deepening scandal of Watergate and the recent resignation of Vice President Spiro Agnew, who had become a hero to many conservatives.

There was a growing feeling on the right that the conservatives needed to regroup, reorganize and recapture the sense of identity and mission that had animated the conservative movement 10 years earlier in the successful struggle to nominate Barry Goldwater.

In sounding out a number of conservative leaders as to what theme he should sound in his address, Reagan was told by some of them that he should elevate the eyes of his audience above the squalor and scandal of Watergate to the principles that inspired the movement — and indeed the nation — in the first place.

The Governor responded with a lyrical address evoking the spirit of the nation's Founders, ending with a quotation from John Winthrop, that the pilgrims' home in the New World should be as a "city set upon a hill." Reagan has repeated the quotation many times since, sometimes rendering it as "a shining city on a hill."

Given his identification with the quotation, it seemed an appropriate title for this collection of speeches.

1

THERE ARE THREE MEN here tonight I am very proud to introduce. It was a year ago this coming February when this country had its spirits lifted as they have never been lifted in many years. This happened when planes began landing on American soil and in the Philippines, bringing back men who had lived with honor for many miserable years in North Vietnam prisons. Three of those men are here tonight, John McCain, Bill Lawrence and Ed Martin.

It is an honor to be here tonight. I am proud that you asked me and I feel more than a little humble in the presence of this distinguished company.

There are men here tonight who, through their wisdom, their foresight and their courage, have earned the right to be regarded as prophets of our philosophy. Indeed they are prophets of our times. In years past when others were silent or too blind to the facts, they spoke up forcefully and fearlessly for what they believed to be right. A decade has passed since Barry Goldwater walked a lonely path across this land reminding us that even a land as rich as ours can't go on forever borrowing against the future, leaving a legacy of debt for another generation and causing a runaway inflation to erode the savings and reduce the standard of living. Voices have been raised trying to rekindle in our country all of the great ideas and principles which set this nation apart from all the others that preceded it, but louder and more strident voices utter easily-sold cliches.

Cartoonists with acid-tipped pens portray some of the reminders of our heritage and our destiny as old-fashioned. They say that we are trying to retreat into a past that actually never existed. Looking to the past in an effort to keep our country from repeating the errors of history is termed by them as taking the country back to McKinley. Of course I never found that was so bad—under McKinley we freed Cuba. On the span of history, we are still thought of as a young upstart country celebrating soon, only our second century as a nation, and yet we are the oldest continuing republic in the world.

I thought that tonight, rather than talking on the subjects you are discussing, or trying to find something new to say, it might be appropriate to reflect a bit on our *heritage*.

You can call it mysticism if you want to, but I have always believed that there was some divine plan that placed this great continent between two oceans to be sought out by those who were possessed of an abiding love of freedom and a special kind of courage.

This was true of those who pioneered the great wilderness in the beginning of this country, as it is also true of those later immigrants who were willing to leave the land of their birth and come to a land where even the language was unknown to them. Call it chauvinistic, but our heritage does not set us apart. Some years ago a writer, who happened to be an avid student of history, told me a story about that day in the little hall in Philadelphia where honorable men, hard-pressed by a King who was flouting the very law they were willing to obey, debated whether they should take the fateful step of declaring their independence from that King. I was told by this man that the story could be found in the writings of Jefferson. I confess, I never researched or made an effort to verify it. Perhaps it is only legend. But story, or legend, he described the atmosphere, the strain, the debate, and that as men for the first time faced the consequences of such an irretrievable act, the walls resounded with the dread word of treason and its price—the gallows and the headman's axe. As the day wore on the issue hung in the balance, and then, according to the story, a man rose in the small gallery. He was not a young man and was obviously calling on all the energy he could muster. Citing the grievances that had brought them to this moment he said, "sign that parchment. They may turn every tree into a gallows, every home into a grave and yet the words of that parchment can never die. For the mechanic in his workshop, they will be words of hope, to the slave in the mines — freedom." And he added, "if my hands were freezing in death, I would sign that parchment with my last ounce of strength. Sign, sign if the next moment the noose is around your neck, sign even if the hall is ringing with the sound of headman's axe, for that parchment will be the textbook of freedom, the bible of the rights of man forever." And then it is said he fell back exhausted. But 56 delegates, swept by his eloquence, signed the Declaration of Independence, a document destined

3

to be as immortal as any work of man can be. And according to the story when they turned to thank him for his timely oratory, he could not be found nor were there any who knew who he was or how he had come in or gone out through the locked and guarded doors.

Well, as I say, whether story or legend, the signing of the document that day in Independence Hall was miracle enough. Fifty six men, a little band so unique—we have never seen their like since—pledged their lives, their fortunes and their sacred honor. Sixteen gave their lives, most gave their fortunes and all of them preserved their sacred honor. What manner of men were they? Certainly they were not an unwashed, revolutionary rebel, nor were then adventurers in a heroic mood. Twenty four were lawyers and jurists, 11 were merchants and tradesmen, nine were farmers. They were men who would achieve security but valued freedom more.

And what price did they pay? John Hart was driven from the side of his desperately ill wife. After more than a year of living almost as an animal in the forest and in caves, he returned to find his wife had died and his children had vanished. He never saw them again, his property was destroyed and he died of a broken heart—but with no regret, only pride in the part he had played that day in Independence Hall. Carter Braxton of Virginia lost all his ships—they were sold to pay his debts. He died in rags. So it was with Ellery, Clymer, Hall, Walton, Gwinnett, Rutledge,, Morris, Livingston, and Middleton. Nelson, learning that Cornwallis was using his home for a headquarters, personally begged Washington to fire on him and destroy his home—he died bankrupt. It has never been reported that any of these men ever expressed bitterness or renounced thier action as not worth the price. Fifty six rank and file ordinary citizens had founded a nation that grew from sea to shining sea, five million farms, quiet villages, cities that never sleep—all done without an area redevelopment plan, urban renewal or a rural legal assistance program.

Now we are a nation of 211 million people with a pedigree that includes blood lines from every corner of the world. We have shed that American-melting-pot blood in every corner of

4

the world, usually in defense of someone's freedom. Those who remained of that remarkable band we call our *Founding Fathers* tied up some of the loose ends about a dozen years after the revolution. It had been the first revolution in all man's history that did not just exchange one set of rulers for another. This had been a philosophical revolution. The culmination of men's dreams for six thousand years were formalized with the Constitution, probably the most unique document ever drawn in the long history of man's relation to man. I know there have been other constitutions, new ones are being drawn today by newly emerging nations. Most of them, even the one of the Soviet Union, contains many of the same guarantees as our own Constitution, and *still* there is a difference. The difference is so subtle that we often overlook it, but is is so great that it tells the whole story. Those other constitutions say "Government grants you these rights" and our's says "you are born with these rights, they are yours by the grace of God, and no government on earth can take them from you."

Lord Acton of England who once said "power corrupts, and absolute power corrupts absolutely," would say of that document "they had solved with astonishing ease and unduplicated success two problems which had heretofore baffled the capacity of the most enlightened nations. They had contrived a system of federal government which prodigiously increased national power and yet respected local liberties and authorities and, they had founded it on a principle of equality without surrendering the securities of property or freedom." Never in any society has the preeminence of the individual been so firmly established and given such a priority.

In less than twenty years we would go to war because the God-given rights of the American sailors, as defined in the constitution, were being violated by a foreign power. We served notice then on the World that all of us together would act collectively to safeguard the rights of even the least among us. But still, in an older cynical world, they were not convinced. The great powers of Europe still had the idea that one day this great continent would be open again to colonizing and they would come over and divide us up.

5

In the meantime men who yearned to breathe free were making their way to our shores. Among them was a young refugee from the Austro-Hungarian Empire. He had been a leader in an attempt to free Hungary from Austrian rule. The attempt had failed and he fled to escape execution. In America, this young Hungarian, Koscha by name, became an importer by trade and took out his first citizenship papers. One day business took him to a Mediterranean port. There was a large Austrian warship under the command of an Admiral in the harbor. He had a manservant with him. He had described to this manservant what the flag of his new country looked like. Word was passed to the Austrian warship that this revolutionary was there and in the night he was kidnapped and taken aboard that large ship. This man's servant, desperate, walking up and down the harbor suddenly spied a flag that resembled the description he had heard. It was a small American war sloop. He went aboard and told Captain Ingraham, of that war sloop his story. Captain Ingraham went to the American Consul. When the American Consul learned that Koscha had only taken out his first citizenship papers, the consul washed his hands of the incident. Captain Ingraham said "I am the senior officer in this port and I believe, under my oath of my office, that I owe this man the protection of our flag."

He went aboard the Austrian warship and demanded to see their prisoner, our citizen. The Admiral was amused, but they brought the man on deck. He was in chains and had been badly beaten. Captain Ingraham said, "I can hear him better without those chains," and the chains were removed. He walked over and said to Kocha, "I will ask you one question, consider your answer carefully. Do you ask the protection of the American flag?" Kocha nodded dumbly "yes," and the Captain said, "you shall have it." He went back and told the frightened consul what he had done. Later in the day three more Austrian ships sailed into harbor. It looked as though the four were getting ready to leave. Captain Ingraham sent a junior officer over to the Austrian flag ship to tell the Admiral that any attempt to leave that harbor with our citizen aboard would be resisted with appropriate force. He said that he would expect a

6

satisfactory answer by four o'clock that afternoon. As the hour neared they looked at each other through the glasses. As it struck four he had them roll the cannons into the ports and had then light the tapers with which they would set off the cannons— one little sloop. Suddenly the lookout tower called out and said "they are lowering a boat," and they rowed Koscha over to the little American ship.

Captain Ingraham then went below and wrote his letter of resignation to the United States Navy. In it he said, "I did what I thought my oath of office required, but if I have embarrassed my country in any way, I resign." His resignation was refused in the United States Senate with these words: "This battle that was never fought may turn out to be the most important battle in our Nation's history." Incidentally, there is to this day, and I hope there always will be, a *USS Ingraham* in the United States Navy.

I did not tell that story out of any desire to be narrowly chauvinistic or to glorify aggressive militarism, but it is an example of government meeting its highest responsibility.

In recent years we have been treated to a rash of noble-sounding phrases. Some of them sound good, but they don't hold up under close analysis. Take for instance the slogan so frequently uttered by the young senator from Massachusetts, "the greatest good for the greatest number." Certainly under that slogan, no modern day Captain Ingraham would risk even the smallest craft and crew for a single citizen. Every dictator who ever lived has justified the enslavement of his people on the theory of what was good for the majority.

We are not a warlike people. Nor is our history filled with tales of aggressive adventures and imperialism — which might come as a shock to some of the placard painters in our modern demonstrations.

The lesson of Vietnam, I think, should be that never again will young Americans be asked to fight and possibly die for a cause unless that cause is so meaningful that we, as a nation, pledge our full resources to achieve victory as quickly as possible.

I realize that such a pronouncement, of course, would possibly be laying one open to the charge of warmongering—but that would also be ridiculous. My generation has paid a higher price and has fought harder for freedom that any generation that had ever lived. We have known four wars in a single lifetime. All were horrible, all could have been avoided if at a particular moment in time we had made it plain that we subscribed to the words of John Stewart Mill when he said that "war is an ugly thing, but not the ugliest of things."

The decayed and degraded state of moral and patriotic feeling which thinks, "nothing is worth a war" is worse. The man who has nothing which he cares about more than his personal safety is a miserable creature and has no chance of being free unless made and kept so by the exertions of better men than himself.

The widespread disaffection with things military is only a part of the *philosophical division* in our land today. I must say to you who have recently, or presently are still recieving an education, I am awed by your powers of resistance. I have some knowledge of the attempts that have been made in many classrooms and lecture halls to persuade you that there is little to admire in America. For the second time in this century, capitalism and the free enterprise are under assault. Privately-owned business is blamed for spoiling the environment, exploiting the worker and seducing, if not outright raping, the customer. Those who make the charge have the solution, of course—government regulation and control. We may never get around to explaining how citizens who are so gullible that they can be suckered into buying cereal or soap that they don't need and would not be good for them, can at the same time be astute enough to choose representatives in government to which they would entrust the running of their lives.

Not too long ago, a poll was taken on 2,500 college campuses in this country. Thousands and thousands of responses were obtained. Overwhelmingly, 65, 70, and 75 per cent of the students found business responsible, as I have said before, for the things that were wrong in this country. That same number said that government was the solution and should take over the management and the control of private business. Eighty per

8

cent of the respondents said they wanted government to keep its paws out of their private lives.

We are told every day that the assembly-line worker is becoming a dull-witted robot and that mass production results in standardization. Well there isn't a socialist country in the world that would not give its copy of Karl Marx for our standardization.

Standardization means production for the masses and the assembly line means more leisure for the worker—freedom from backbreaking and mind-dulling drudgery that man had known for centuries past. Karl Marx did not abolish child labor or free the women from working in the coal mines in England—the steam engine and modern machinery did that.

Unfortunately, the disciples of the new order have had a hand in determining to much policy in recent decades. Government has grown in size and power and cost through the New Deal, the Fair Deal, the New Frontier and the Great Society. It cost more for government today than a family pays for food, shelter and clothing combined. Not even the Office of Management and Budget knows how many boards, commissions, bureaus and agencies there are in the federal government, but the federal registry, listing their regulations, is just a few pages short of being as big as the Encyclopedia Britannica.

During the Great Society we saw the greatest growth of this government—there were eight cabinet departments and 12 independent agencies to administer the federal health program. There were 35 housing programs and 20 transportation projects. Public utilities had to cope with 27 different agencies on just routine business. There were 192 installations and nine departments with 1,000 projects having to do with the field of pollution.

One Congressman found the federal government was spending $4 billion on research in its own laboratories but did not know where they were, how many people were working in them, or what they were doing. One of the reseach projects was "the demography of happiness," and for $249,000 we found that "people who make more money are happier than people who make less, young people are happier than old people, and people who are healthier are happier than people who are sick."

For 15 cents they could have bought an Almanac and read the old bromide, "it's better to be rich, young and healthy, than poor, old and sick."

The course that you have chosen is far more in tune with the hopes and aspirations of our people, than are those who would sacrifice freedom for some fancied security.

Standing on the tiny deck of the *Arabella* in 1630 off the Massachusetts coast, John Winthrop said "we will be as a city upon a hill. The eyes of all people are upon us, so that if we deal falsely with our God in this work we have undertaken and so cause Him to withdraw His present help from us, we shall be made a story and a byword throughout the world." Well, we have *not* dealt falsely with our God, even if He *is* temporarily suspended from the classroom.

When I was born my life expectancy was 10 years less than I have already lived—that's a cause of regret for some people in California, I know. Ninety per cent of Americans at that time lived beneath what is considered the poverty line today, three-quarters lived in what is considered substandard housing. Today each of those figures is less than 10 per cent. We have increased our life expectancy by wiping out, almost totally, diseases that still ravage mankind in other parts of the world. I doubt if the young people here tonight know the names of some of the diseases that were commonplace when we were growing up. We have more doctors per thousand people than any nation in the world. We have more hospitals that any nation in the world.

When I was your age, believe it or not, none of us knew that we even had a racial problem. When I graduated from college and became a radio sport announcer, broadcasting major league baseball, I didn't have a Hank Aaron or a Willie Mays to talk about. The Spaulding Guide said baseball was a game for Caucasian gentlemen. Some of us then began editorializing and campaigning against this. Gradually we campaigned against all those other areas where the *constitutional rights* of a large segment of our citizenry were being denied. We have not finished the job. We still have a long way to go, but we have made more progress in a few years than we have made in more than a century.

10

One third of all the students in the world who are pursuing higher education are doing so in the United States. The percentage of our young Negro community that is going to college is greater than the percentage of whites in any other country in the world.

One half of all the economic activity in the entire history of man has taken place in this Republic. We have distributed out wealth more widely among our people than any society known to man. Americans work less hours for a higher standard of living than any other people. Ninety five per cent of all our families have an adequate daily intake of nutrients—and a part of the five per cent that don't are trying to lose weight! Ninety nine per cent have gas or electric refrigeration, 92 per cent have televisions, and an equal number have telephones. There are 120 million cars on our streets and highways—and all of them are on the street at once when you are trying to get home at night. But isn't this just proof of our materialism — the very thing that we are charged with? Well, we also have more churches, more libraries, we support voluntarily more symphony orchestras, and opera companies, non-profit theatres, and publish more books than all the other nations of the world put together.

Somehow America has bred a kindliness into our people un-matched anywhere, as has been pointed out in that best-selling record by a Canadian journalist. We are not a sick society. A sick society could not produce the men that set foot on the moon, or who are now circling the earth above us in the skylab. A sick society bereft of morality and courage did not produce the men who went through those year of torture and captivity in Vietnam. Where did we find such men? They are typical of this land as the Founding Fathers were typical. We found them in our streets, in the offices, the shops and the working places of our country and on the farms.

We cannot escape out *destiny* nor should we try to do so. The leadership of the free world was thrust upon us two centuries ago in that little hall of Philadelphia. In the days followed World War II, when the economic strength and power *of America* was all that stood between the world and the return to the dark ages,

11

Pope Pius XII said "the American people have a great genius for splendid and unselfish actions. Into the hands of America God has placed the destinies of an afflicted mankind."

We are indeed, and we are today, the last best hope of man on earth.

II

Let Them Go Their Way
MARCH 1, 1975

Governor Reagan's speech to the second CPAC confer-
ence in February was much different from the first.
Richard Nixon had resigned the Presidency the preceding
August and Vice President Gerald Ford now occupied the
Oval Office.

The new President's relations with conservatives had
quickly soured, due mainly to the appointment of a host of
moderate and liberal Republicans to key offices in the new
Administration. The most offensive of these was President
Ford's nomination of Nelson Rockefeller to be Vice President. Governor Rockefeller was the *bete noir* of the GOP
right, which had fought him for control over the Party
since 1964, and his selection infuriated the GOP's conservative rank and file.

So deep was the disenchantment with the Rockefeller
choice that many conservative activists and leaders talked
of leaving the GOP and forming a new political party. The
third-party option was, in fact, the main topic of discussion at the 1975 CPAC and intense speculation was
focused on Governor Reagan's thinking on the matter, the
consensus being that his active support would be necessary
to make the new party option viable. In this address the
Governor announced his intention to remain in the
Republican Party and to work to re-shape the GOP as a
truly conservative party.

S INCE OUR LAST MEETING we have been through a disastrous
election. It is easy for us to be discouraged, as pundits hail

that election as a repudiation of our philosophy and even as a mandate of some kind or other. But the signifiance of the election was not registered by those who voted, but by those who stayed home. If there was anything like a mandate it will be found among almost two-thirds of the citizens who refused to participate.

Bitter as it is to accept the results of the November election, we should have reason for some optimism. For many years now we have preached "the gospel," in opposition to the philosophy of so-called liberalism which was, in truth, a call to collectivism.

Now, it is possible we have been persuasive to a greater degree than we had ever realized. Few, if any, Democratic party candidates in the last election ran as liberals. Listening to them I had the eerie feeling we were hearing reruns of Goldwater speeches. I even thought I heard a few of my own.

Bureaucracy was assailed and fiscal responsibility hailed. Even George McGovern donned sackcloth and ashes and did penance for the good people of South Dakota.

But let's not be so naive as to think we are witnessing a mass conversion to the principles of conservatism. Once sworn into office, the victors reverted to type. In their view, apparently the ends justified the means.

The "Young Turks" had campaigned against "evil politicians." They turned against committee chairmen of their own party, displaying a taste and talent as cutthroat power politicians quite in contrast to their campaign rhetoric and idealism. Still, we must not forget that they molded their campaigning to fit what even they recognized was the mood of the majority. And we must see to it that the people are reminded of this as they now pursue their ideological goals—and pursue them they will.

I know you are aware of the national polls which show that a greater (and increasing) number of Americans—Republicans, Democrats and independents—classify themselves as "conservatives" than ever before. And a poll of rank-and-file union members reveals dissatisfaction with the amount of power their own leaders have assumed, and a resentment of their use of that power for partisan politics. Would it shock you to know that in that poll 68 per cent of rank-and-file union members of this

14

country came out endorsing right-to-work legislation?

These polls give cause for some optimism, but at the same time reveal a confusion that exists and the need for a continued effort to "spread the word."

In another recent survey, of 35,000 college and university students polled, three-fourths blame American business and industry for all of our economic and social ills. The same three-fourths think the answer is more (and virtually complete) regimentation and government control of all phases of business— including the imposition of wage and price controls. Yet, 80 per cent in the same poll want less government interference in their own lives!

In 1972 the people of this country had a clear-cut choice, based on the issues—to a greater extent than any election in half a century. In overwhelming numbers they ignored party labels, not so much to vote for a man or even a policy as to repudiate a philosophy. In doing so they repudiated that final step into the welfare state—that call for the confiscation and redistribution of their earnings on a scale far greater that what we now have. They repudiated the abandonment of national honor and a weakening of this nation's ability to protect itself.

A study has been made that is so revealing that I'm not surprised it has been ignored by a certain number of political commentators and columnists. The Political Science Department of Georgetown University researched the mandate of the 1972 election and recently presented its findings at a seminar.

Taking several major issues which, incidentally, are still the issues of the day, they polled rank-and-file members of the Democratic party on their approach to these problems. Then they polled the delegates to the two major national conventions —the leaders of the parties.

They found the delegates to the Republican convention almost identical in their responses to those of the rank-and-file Republicans. Yet, the delegates to the Democratic convention were miles apart from the thinking of their own party members.

The mandate of 1972 still exists. The people of America have been confused and disturbed by events since that election, but they hold an unchanged philosophy.

15

Our task is to make them see that what we represent is identical to their own hopes and dreams of what America can and should be. If there are questions as to whether the principles of conservatism hold up in practice, we have the answers to them. Where conservative principles have been tried, they have worked.

Gov. Meldrim Thomson is making them work in New Hampshire; so is Arch Moore in West Virginia and Mills Godwin in Virginia. Jack Williams made them work in Arizona and I'm sure Jim Edwards will in South Carolina.

If you will permit me, I can recount my own experience in California.

When I went to Sacramento eight years ago, I had the belief that government was no deep, dark mystery; that it could be operated efficiently by using the same common sense practiced in our everyday life, in our homes, in business and private affairs.

The "lab test" of my theory—California—was pretty messed up after eight years of a roadshow version of the Great Society. Our first and only briefing came from the outgoing director of finance who said, "We're spending $1 million more a day than we're taking in. I have a golf date. Good luck!" That was the most cheerful news we were to hear for quite some time.

California state government was increasing by about 5,000 new employees a year. We were the welfare capital of the world with 16 per cent of the nation's caseload. Soon, California's caseload was increasing by 40,000 a month.

We turned to the people themselves for help. Two hundred and fifty experts in the various fields volunteered to serve on task forces at no cost to the taxpayers. They went into every department of state government and came back with 1,800 recommendations on how modern business practices could be used to make government more efficient. We adopted 1,600 of them.

We instituted a policy of "cut, squeeze and trim" and froze the hiring of employees as replacements for retiring employees or others leaving state service.

After a few years of struggling with the professional welfarists

16

we again turned to the people. First, we obtained another task force and, when the legislature refused to help implement its recommendations, we presented the recommendations to the electorate.

It still took some doing. The legislature insisted our reforms would not work; that the needy would starve in the streets; that the workload would be dumped on the counties; that property taxes would go up and that we'd run up a deficit the first year of $750 million.

That was four years ago. Today, the needy have had an average increase of 43 per cent in welfare grants in California, but the taxpayers have saved $2 billion by the caseload not increasing that 40,000 a month. Instead, there are some 400,000 fewer on welfare today than then.

Forty of the state's 58 counties have reduced property taxes for two years in a row (some for three). That $750-million deficit turned into an $850-million surplus which we returned to the people in a one-time tax rebate. That wasn't easy. One state senator described that rebate as ''an unnecessary expenditure of public funds.''

For more than two decades governments—federal, state, local—have been increasing in size two-and-a-half times faster than the population increase. In the last 10 years they have increased in cost the payroll seven times as fast as the increase in numbers.

We have just turned over to a new administration in Sacramento a government virtually the same size it was eight years ago. With the state's growth rate, this means that government absorbed a workload increase, in some departments as much as 66 per cent.

We also turned over—for the first time in almost a quarter of a century—a balanced budget and a surplus of $500 million. In these eight years just passed, we returned to the people in rebates, tax reductions and bridge toll reductions $5.7 billion. All of this is contrary to the will of those who deplore conservatism and profess to be liberals, yet all of it is pleasing to its citizenry.

Make no mistake, the leadership of the Democratic party is still out of step with the majority of Americans.

17

Speaker Carl Albert recently was quoted as saying that our problem is "60 per cent recession, 30 per cent inflation and 10 per cent energy." That makes as much sense as saying two and two make 22.

Without inflation there would be no recession. And unless we curb inflation we can see the end of our society and economic system. The painful fact is we can only halt inflation by undergoing a period of economic dislocation—a recession, if you will.

We can take steps to ease the suffering of some who will be hurt more than others, but if we turn from fighting inflation and adopt a program only to fight recession we are on the road to disaster.

In his first address to Congress, the President asked Congress to join him in an all-out effort to balance the budget. I think all of us wish that he had re-issued that speech instead of this year's budget message.

What side can be taken in a debate over whether the deficit should be $52 billion or $70 billion or $80 billion preferred by the profligate Congress?

Inflation has one cause and one cause only: government spending more than government takes in. And the cure to inflation is a balanced budget. We know of course that after 40 yers of social tinkering and Keynesian experimentation that we can't do this all at once, but it can be achieved. Balancing the budget is like protecting your virtue: you have to learn to say "no."

This is no time to repeat the shopworn panaceas of the New Deal, the Fair Deal and the Great Society. John Kenneth Galbraith, who, in my opinion, is living proof that economics is an inexact science, has written a new book. It is called *Economics and the Public Purpose*. In it, he asserts that market arrangements in our economy have given us inadequate housing, terrible mass transit, poor health care and a host of other miseries. And then, for the first time to my knowledge, he advances socialism as the answer to our problems.

Shorn of all side issues and extraneous matter, the problem underlying all others is the worldwide contest for the hearts and minds of mankind. Do we find the answers to human misery in freedom as it is known, or do we sink into the deadly dullness of the Socialist antheap?

Those who suggest that the latter is some kind of solution are, I think, open to challenge. Let's have no more theorizing when actual comparison is possible. There is in the world a great nation, larger than ours in territory and populated with 250 million capable people. It is rich in resources and has had more than 50 uninterrupted years to practice socialism without opposition.

We could match them, but it would take a little doing on our part. We'd have to cut our paychecks back by 75 per cent; move 60 million workers back to the farm; abandon two-thirds of our steel-making capacity; destroy 40 million television sets; tear up 14 of every 15 miles of highway; junk 19 of every 20 automobiles; tear up two-thirds of our railroad track; knock down 70 per cent of our houses; and rip out nine out of every 10 telephones. Then, all we have to do is find a capitalist country to sell us wheat on credit to keep us from starving!

Our people are in a time of discontent. Our vital energy supplies are threatened by possibly the most powerful cartel in human history. Our traditional allies in Western Europe are experiencing political and economic instability bordering on chaos.

We seem to be increasingly alone in a world grown more hostile, but we let our defenses shrink to pre-Pearl Harbor levels. And we are conscious that in Moscow the crash buildup of arms continues. The SALT II agreement in Vladivostok, if not renegotiated, guarantees the Soviets a clear missile superiority sufficient to make a "first strike" possible with little fear of reprisal. Yet, too many congressmen demand further cuts in our own defenses, including delay if not cancellation of the B-1 bomber.

I realize that millions of Americans are sick of hearing about Indochina, and perhaps it is politically unwise to talk of our obligation to Cambodia and South Vietnam. But we pledged —in an agreement that brought our men home and freed our prisoners—to give our allies arms and ammunition to replace on a one-for-one basis what they expend in resisting the aggression of the Communists who are violating the cease-fire and are fully aided by their Soviet and Red Chinese allies. Congress has already reduced the appropriation to half of what they need and threatens to reduce it even more.

Can we live with ourselves if we, as a nation, betray our friends and ignore our pledged word? And, if we do, who would ever trust us again? To consider committing such an act so contrary to our deepest ideals is symptomatic of the erosion of standards and values. And this adds to our discontent.

We did not seek world leadership; it was thrust upon us. It has been our destiny almost from the first moment this land was settled. If we fail to keep our rendezvous with destiny or, as John Winthrop said in 1630, "Deal falsely with our God," we shall be made "A story and byword throughout the world."

Americans are hungry to feel once again a sense of mission and greatness.

I don't know about you, but I am impatient with those Republicans who after the last election rushed into print saying, "we must broaden the base of our party"—when what they meant was to fuzz up and blur even more the differences between ourselves and our opponents.

It was a feeling that there was not a sufficient difference now between the parties that kept a majority of the voters away from the polls. When have we ever advocated a closed-door policy? Who has ever been barred from participating?

Our people look for a cause to believe in. Is it a third party we need, or is it a new and revitalized second party, raising a banner of no pale pastels, but bold colors which make it unmistakably clear where we stand on all of the issues troubling the people.

Let us show that we stand for fiscal integrity and sound money and above all for an end to deficit spending, with ultimate retirement of the national debt.

Let us also include a permanent limit on the percentage of the people's earnings government can take without their consent.

Let our banner proclaim a genuine tax reform that will begin by simplifying the income tax so that workers can compute their obligation without having to employ legal help.

And let it provide indexing—adjusting the brackets to the cost of living—so that an increase in salary merely to keep pace with inflation does not move the taxpayer into a surtax bracket. Failure to provide this means an increase in government's share and would make the worker worse off than he was before he got the raise.

Let our banner proclaim our belief in a free market as the greatest provider for the people. Let us also call for an end to the nitpicking, the harassment and overregulation of business and industry which restricts expansion and our ability to compete in world markets.

Let us explore ways to ward off socialism, not by increasing government's coercive power, but by increasing participation by the people in the ownership of our industrial machine.

Our banner must recognize the responsibility of government to protect the law-abiding, holding those who commit misdeeds personally accountable.

And we must make it plain to international adventurers that our love of peace stops short of "peace at any price."

We will maintain whatever level of strength is necessary to preserve our free way of life.

A political party cannot be all things to all people. It must represent certain fundamental beliefs which must not be compromised to political expediency, or simply to swell its numbers.

I do not believe I have proposed anything that is contrary to what has been considered Republican principle. It is at the same time the very basis of conservatism. It is time to reassert that principle and raise it to full view. And if there are those who cannot subscribe to these principles, then let them go their way.

III

The New Republican Party: 'I Have Seen the Conservative Future And It Works!'

FEBRUARY 6, 1977

Governor Reagan's next CPAC address followed close on the heels of Jimmy Carters inauguration as President. Mr. Reagan had not appeared at the 1976 conference because, as he put it wryly, he "had some business in New Hampshire that wouldn't wait."

The "business" was the New Hampshire Primary which he lost narrowly to President Gerald Ford. After a hard-fought series of primaries and caucuses the President edged out Governor Reagan for the Republican nomination at a closely divided and tumultuous convention in Kansas City. Mr. Ford thereupon lost the White House in an equally hard-fought and close election to Governor Jimmy Carter of Georgia.

Though he lost the nomination to President Ford, Governor Reagan emerged from the 1976 election as the heavy favorite for the GOP nomination in 1980.

It was his belief—a belief shared by many GOP leaders who had backed Ford over Reagan—that the American people were basically conservative and that the Republican Party would have won in 1976 if it had held aloft the banner of "bold colors"—of conservative principles.

In his 1977 CPAC speech Governor Reagan challenged his conservative followers to act on those principles in shaping not a new third party, but a "New Republican Party"—one that he, by clear implication, was ready to lead.

22

The wildly enthusiastic reception given the Governor and Mrs. Reagan by the largest CPAC audience to date made it plain that, as far as conservative activists were concerned, the 1980 campaign was already underway and Reagan was their man.

I'M HAPPY TO BE BACK WITH YOU in this annual event after missing last year's meeting. I had some business in New Hampshire that wouldn't wait.

Three weeks ago here in our Nation's Capital I told a group of conservative scholars that we are currently in the midst of a reordering of the political realities that have shaped our time. We know today that the principles and values that lie at the heart of conservatism are shared by the majority.

Despite what some in the press may say, we who are proud to call ourselves "conservative" are not a minority of a minority party; we are part of the great majority of Americans of both major parties and of most of the Independents as well.

A Harris poll released September 7, 1975 showed 18 per cent identifying themselves as liberal and 31 per cent as conservative, with 41 per cent as middle of the road; a few months later, on January 5, 1976, by a 43–19 plurality those polled by Harris said they would "prefer to see the country move in a more conservative direction than a liberal one."

Last October 24th, the Gallup organization released the result of a poll taken right in the midst of the presidential campaign.

Respondents were asked to state where they would place themselves on a scale ranging from "right-of-center" (which was defined as "conservative") to left-of-center (which was defined as "liberal").

• thirty-seven per cent viewed themselves as left of center or liberal.

• twelve per cent placed themselves in the middle

• fifty-one per cent said they were right of center, that is, conservative.

What I find interesting about this particular poll is that it offered those polled a range of choices on a left–right continuum. This seems to me to be a more realistic approach than dividing the world into strict left and rights. Most of us, I guess, like to think of ourselves as avoiding both extremes, and the fact that a majority of Americans chose one or the other position on the right end of the spectrum is really impressive.

Those polls confirm that most Americans are basically conservative in their outlook. But once we have said this, we conservatives have not *solved* our problems, we have merely stated them clearly. Yes, conservatism can and does mean different things to those who call themselves conservatives.

You know, as I do, that most commentators make a distinction between they call "social" conservatism and "economic" conservatism. The so-called social issues — law and order, abortion, busing, quota systems — are usually associated with blue-collar, ethnic and religious groups themselves traditionally associated with the Democratic Party. The economic issues — inflation, deficit spending and big government—are usually associated with Republican Party members and independents who concentrate their attention on economic matters.

Now I am willing to accept this view of two major kinds of conservatism — or, better still, two different conservative constituencies. But at the same time let me say that the old lines that once clearly divided these two kinds of conservatism are disappearing.

In fact, the time has come to see if it is possible to present a program of action based on political principle that can attract those interested in the so-called "social" issues and those interested in "economic" issues. In short, isn't it possible to combine the two major segments of contemporary American conservatism into one politically effective whole?

I believe the answer is: Yes, it *is* possible to create a political entity that will reflect the views of the great, hitherto, conservative majority. We went a long way toward doing it in California. We can do it in America. This is not a dream, a wistful hope. It is and has been a reality. I have seen the conservative future and it works!

Let me say again what I said to our conservative friends from

24

the academic world: What I envision is not simply a melding together of the two branches of American conservatism into a temporary uneasy alliance, but the creation of a new, lasting majority.

This will mean compromise. But not a compromise of basic principle. What will emerge will be something new; something open and vital and dynamic, something the great conservative majority will recognize as its own, because at the heart of this undertaking is principled politics.

I have always been puzzled by the inability of some political and media types to understand exactly what is meant by adherence to political principle. All too often in the press and the television evening news it is treated as a call for "ideological purity." Whatever ideology may mean—and it seems to mean a variety of things, depending upon who is using it — it always conjures up in my mind a picture of a rigid, irrational clinging to abstract theory in the face of reality. We have to recognize that in this country "ideology" is a scare-word. And, for good reason. Marxist–Leninism is, to give but one example, an ideology. All the facts of the real world have to be fitted to the Procrustean bed of Marx and Lenin. If the facts don't happen to fit the ideology, the facts are chopped off and dicarded.

I consider this to be the complete opposite to principled conservatism. If there is any political viewpoint in this world which is free for slavish adherence to abstraction, it is American conservatism.

When a conservative states that the free market is the best mechanism ever devised by the mind of man to meet material needs, he is merely stating what a careful examination of the real world has told him is the truth.

When a conservative says that totalitarian Communism is an absolute enemy of human freedom he is not theorizing — he is reporting the ugly reality captured so unforgettably in the writings of Alexander Solzhenitsyn.

When a conservative says it is bad for the government to spend more than it takes in, he is simply showing the same common sense that tells him to come in out of the rain.

When a conservative says that busing does not work, he is not

25

appealing to some theory of education—he is merely reporting what he has seen down at the local school.

When a conservative quotes Jefferson that government that is closest to the people is best, it is because he knows that Jefferson risked his life, his fortune and his sacred honor to make certain that what he and his fellow patriots learned from experience was not crushed by an ideology of empire.

Conservatism is the antithesis of the kind of ideological fanatacism that has brought so much horror and destruction to the world. The common sense and common decency of ordinary men and women, working out their own lives in their own way—this is the heart of American conservatism today. Conservative wisdom and principles are derived from willingness to learn, not just from what is going on *now*, but from what has happened before.

The principles of conservatism are sound because they are based on what men and women have discovered through experience in not just one generation or a dozen, but in all the combined experience of mankind. When we conservatives say that we know something about political affairs, and that we know can be stated as principles, we are saying that the principles we hold dear are those that have been found, through experience, to be ultimately beneficial for individuals, for families, for communities and for nations—found through the often bitter testing of pain, or sacrifice and sorrow.

One thing that must be made clear in post-Watergate is this: the American new conservative majority we represent is *not* based on abstract theorizing of the kind that turns off the American people, but on common sense, intelligence, reason, hard work, faith in God, and the guts to say, yes, there *are* things we do strongly believe in, that we are willing to live for, and yes, if necessary, to die for. That is not "ideological purity." It is simply what built this country and kept it great.

Let us lay to rest, once and for all, the myth of a small group of ideological purists trying to capture a majority. Replace it with the reality of a majority trying to assert its rights against the tryanny of powerful academics, fashionable left-revolutionaries, some economic illiterates who happen to hold elective

26

office and the social engineers who dominate the dialogue and set the format in political and social affairs. If there is any ideological fanaticism in American political life, it is to be found among the enemies of freedom on the left or right—those who would sacrifice principle to theory, those who worship only the god of political, social and economic abstractions, ignoring the realities of everyday life. They are *not* conservatives.

Our first job is to get this message across to those who share most of our principles. If we allow ourselves to be portrayed as ideological shock troops without correcting this error we are doing ourselves and our cause a disservice. Wherever and whenever we can, we should gently but firmly correct our political and media friends who have been perpetuating the myth of conservatism as a narrow ideology. Whatever the word may have meant in the past, today conservatism means principles evolving from experience and a belief in change when necessary, but not just for the sake of change.

One we have established this, the next question is: what will be the political vehicle by which the majority can assert its rights?

I have to say I cannot agree with some of my friends— perhaps including some of you here tonight—who have answered that question by saying this nation needs a new political party.

I respect that view and I know that those who have reached it have done so after long hours of study. But I believe that political success of the principles we believe in can best be achieved in the Republican Party. I believe the Republican Party can hold and should provide the political mechanism through which the goals of the majority of Americans can be achieved. For one thing, the biggest single grouping of conservatives is to be found in that party. It makes more sense to build on that grouping than to break it up and start over. Rather than a third party, we can have a new first party made up of people who share our principles. I have said before that if a formal change in name proves desirable, then so be it. But tonight, for purpose of discussion, I'm going to refer it simply as the New Republican Party.

27

And let me say so there can be no mistakes as to what I mean:
—the New Republican Party I envision will not be, and cannot,
be one limited to the country club–big business image that, for
reasons both fair and unfair, it is burdened with today. The New
Republican Party I am speaking about is going to have room for
the man and the woman in the factories, for the farmer, for the
cop on the beat and the millions of Americans who may never
have thought of joining our party before—but whose interests
coincide with those represented by principled Republicanism. If
we are to attract more working men and women of this country,
we will do so not by simply "making room" for them, but by
making certain they have a say in what goes on in the party. The
Democratic party turned its back on the majority of social conservatives during the 1960s. The New Republican Party of the
late '70s and '80s must welcome them, seek them out, enlist
them, not only as rank-and-file members but as leaders and as
candidates.

The time has come for Republicans to say to black voters:
look, we offer principles that black Americans can, and do, support. We believe in jobs, real jobs; we believe in education that
is really education; we believe in treating all Americans as
individuals and not as stereotypes or voting blocs — and we
believe that the long-range interest of black Americans lies in
looking at what each major party has to offer. And *then* deciding
on the merits. The Democratic Party takes the black vote for
granted. Well, it's time black America and the New Republican
Party move toward each other and create a situation in which no
black vote can be taken for granted.

The New Republican Party I envision is one that will ener-
getically seek out the best candidates for every elective office,
candidates who not only agree with, but understand, and are
willing to fight for a sound, honest economy, for the interests of
American families and neighborhoods and communities and a
strong national defense. And these candidates must be able to
communicate those principles to the American people in language they understand. Inflation isn't a textbook problem. Unemployment isn't a textbook problem. They should be discussed in human terms.

Our candidates must be willing to communicate with every level of society, because the principles we espouse are universal and cut across traditional lines. In every Congressional district there should be a search made for young men and women who share these principles and they should be brought into positions of leadership in the local Republican Party groups. We can find attractive, articulate candidates if we look, and when we find them, we will begin to change the sorry state of affairs that has led a Democratic-controlled Congress for more than 40 years. I need not remind you that you can have the soundest principles in the world, but if you don't have candidates who can communicate those principles, candidate who are articulate as well as principled, you are going to lose election after election. I refuse to believe that the good Lord divided this world into Republicans who defend basic values, and Democrats who win elections. We have to find tough, bright young men and women who are sick and tired of cliches and the pomposity and the mind-numbing economic idiocy of the liberals in Washington.

It is at this point, however, that we come across a question that is really the essential one: what will be the basis of this New Republican Party? To what set of values and principles can our candidates appeal? Where can Americans who want to know where we stand look for guidance?

Fortunately, we have an answer to that question. That answer was provided last summer by the men and women of the Republican Party—not just the leadership, but the ones who have built the party on local levels all across the country.

The answer was provided in the 1976 Platform of the Republican Party.

This was not a document handed down from on high. It was hammered out in free and open debate among all those who care about our party and the principles it stands for.

The Republican Platform is unique. Unlike any other party platform I have ever seen, it answers not only programmatic questions for the immediate future of the party but also provides a clear outline of the underlying principles upon which those programs are based

The New Republican Party can and should use the

29

Republican Platform of 1976 as the major source from which a Declaration of Principles can be created and offered to the American people.

Tonight I want to offer to you my own version of what such a Declaration might look like. I make no claim to originality. This Declaration I propose is relatively short, taken, for most part, word for word from the Republican Platform. It concerns itself with basic principles, not with specific solutions.

We, the members of the New Republican Party, believe that the preservation and enhancement of the values that strengthen and protect individual freedom, family life, communities and neighborhoods and the liberty of our beloved nation should be at the heart of any legislative or political program presented to the American people. Toward that end, we, therefore, commit ourselves to the following propositions and offer them to each American believing that the New Republican Party, based on such principles, will serve the interest of all the American people.

We believe that liberty can be measured by how much freedom Americans have to make their own decisions—even their own mistakes. Government must step in when one's liberties impinge on one's neighbor's. Government must protect constitutional rights, deal with other governments, protect citizens from aggressors, assure equal opportunity, and be compassionate in caring for those citizens who are unable to care for themselves.

Our federal system of local-state-national government is designed to sort out on what level these actions should be taken. Those concerns of a national character—such as air and water pollution that do not respect state boundaries, or the national transportation system, or efforts to safeguard your civil liberties —must, of course, be handled on the national level.

As a general rule, however, we believe that government action should be taken first by the government that resides as close to you as possible.

We also believe that Americans, often acting through voluntary organizations, should have the opportunity to solve many of the social problems of their communities. This spirit of

30

freely helping others is uniquely American and should be encouraged in every way by government.

Families must continue to be the foundation of our nation.

Families—not government programs—are the best way to make sure our children are properly nurtured, our elderly are cared for, our cultural and spiritual heritages are perpetuated, our laws are observed and our values are preserved.

Thus it is imperative that our government's programs, actions, officials and social welfare institutions never be allowed to jeopardize the family. We fear the government may be powerful enough to destroy our families; we know that it is not powerful enough to replace them. The New Republican Party must be committed to working always in the interest of the American family.

Every dollar spent by government is a dollar earned by individuals. Government must always ask: Are your dollars being wisely spent? Can we afford it? Is it not better for the country to leave your dollars in your pocket?

Elected officials, their appointees, and government workers are expected to perform their public acts with honesty, openness, diligence, and special integrity.

Government must work for the goal of justice and the elimination of unfair practices, but no government has yet designed a more productive economic system or one which benefits as many people as the American market system.

The beauty of our land is our legacy to our children. It must be protected by us so that they can pass it on intact to their children.

The United States must always stand for peace and liberty in the world and the rights of the individual. We must form sturdy partnerships with our allies for the preservation of freedom. We must be ever willing to negotiate differences, but equally mindful that there are American ideals that cannot be compromised. Given that there are other nations with potentially hostile design, we recognize that we can reach our goals only while maintaining a superior national defense, second to none.

In his inaugural speech President Carter said that he saw the world "dominated by a new spirit....." He said, and I quote:

31

"The passion for freedom is on the rise...."

Well, I don't know how he knows this, but if it is true, then it is the most unrequited passion in human history. The world is being dominated by a new spirit, all right, but it isn't the spirit of freedom.

It isn't very often you see a familiar object that shocks and frightens you. But the other day I came across a map of the world created by Freedom House, an organization monitoring the state of freedom in the world for the past 25 years. It is an ordinary map, with one exception: it shows the world's nations in white for free, shaded for partly free and black for not free.

Almost all of the great Eurasian land mass is completely colored black, from the western border of East Germany, through middle and eastern Europe, through the awesome spaces of the Soviet Union, on to the Bering Strait in the north, down past the immensity of China, still further, down to Vietnam and the South China Sea—in all that huge sprawling, inconceivably immense area not a single political or personal or religious freedom exists. The entire continent of Africa, from the Mediterranean to the Cape of Good Hope, from the Atlantic to the Indian Ocean, all that vastness is almost totaly unfree. In the tiny nation of Tanzania alone, according to a report in the New York *Times*, there are 3,000 people in detention for political crimes—that is more than the total being held in South Africa! The Mideast has only one free state: Israel. If a visitor from another planet were to approach earth, and if this planet showed free nations in light and unfree nations in darkness, the pitifully small beacons of light would make him wonder what was hidden in that terrifying, enormous blackness.

We know what is hidden: Gulag. Torture. Families — and human beings — broken apart. No free press, no freedom of religion. The ancient forms of tyranny revived and made even more hideous and strong through what Winston Churchill once called "a perverted science." Men rotting for years in solitary confinement because they have different political and economic beliefs, solitary confinement that drives the fortunate ones insane and makes the survivors wish for death.

Only now and then do we in the West hear a voice, from out

of that darkness. Then there is silence — the silence of human slavery. There is no more terrifying sound in human experience; with one possible exception. Look at that map again. The very heart of the darkness is the Soviet Union and from that heart comes a different sound. It is the whirring sound of machinery and the whisper of the computer technology we ourselves have sold them. It is the sound of building; building of the strongest military machine ever devised by man. Our military strategy is designed to hopefully prevent a war. Theirs is designed to win one. A group of eminent scientists, scholars and intelligence experts offer a survey showing that the Soviet Union is driving for military superiority and are derided as hysterically making — quote — "a worst case" — unquote — concerning Soviet intentions and capabilities.

But is it not precisely the duty of the national government to be prepared for the worst case? Two Senators, after studying the North Atlantic Treaty Organization, have reported to the Armed Forces committee that Soviet forces in Eastern Europe have the capability to launch, with little warning, a "potentially devastating" attack in Central Europe from what is termed a "standing alert."

Reading their report, one can almost see the enormous weight of the parts of the earth that are under tyranny shifting in an irresistable tilt toward that tiny portion of land in freedom's light. Even now in Western Europe we have Communists in the government of Italy. France appeasing terrorists, and England — for centuries the model or the sword of freedom in Western Europe — weak, dispirited, turning inward.

A "worst case"? How could you make a *good* case out of the facts as they are known? The Soviet Union, poised on the edge of free Europe, capable of striking from a standing start, has modern tanks in far greater numbers than the outmoded vehicles of NATO. We have taken comfort from NATO's superiority in the air, but now the Soviet Union has made a dramatic swing away from its historic defensive air posture to one capable of supporting offensive action. NATO's southern flank is described in the Senate report with a single word— "shambles."

33

The report is simply reality as it was, with different names and faces, in Europe in the late 1930s when so many refused to believe and thought if we don't look the threat will go away.

We don't want hysteria. We don't want distortion of Soviet power. We want truth. And above all we want peace. And to have that the United States has to immediately re-examine its entire view of the world and develop a strategy of freedom. We cannot be the second best super-power for the simple reason that he who is second is last. In this deadly game, there are no silver medals for second.

President Carter, as a candidate, said he would cut five to seven billion dollars from the defense budget. We must let him know that while we agree there must be no fat in our armed forces those armed forces must be capable of coping with the new reality presented to us by the Russians, and cutting seven billions dollars out of our defense budget is not the way to accomplish this. Some years ago, a young President said we will make any sacrifice, bear any burden and we will to preserve our freedom.

Our relationship with main land China is clouded. The so-called "gang of four" are up one day and down the next and we are seeing the pitfalls of making deals with charismatic personalities and living legends. The charisma fades as the living legends die, and those who take their place are interested not in our best wishes but in power. The key word for China today is turmoil. We should watch and observe and analyze as closely and rationally as we can.

But in our relationships with the mainland of China we should always remember that the conditions and possibilities for and the realities of freedom exist to an infinitely greater degree with our Chinese friends in Taiwan. We can never go wrong if we do what is morally right, and the moral way—the honorable way—is to keep our commitment, our solemn promise to the poeple of Taiwan. Our liberal friends have made much of the lack of freedom in some Latin American countries. Senator Edward Kennedy and his colleagues here in Washington let no opportunity pass to let us know about horrors in Chile.

Well, I think when the United States of America is

considering a deal with a country that hasn't had an election in almost eight years, where the press is under the thumb of a dictatorship, where ordinary citizens are abducted in the night by secret police, where military domination of the country is known to be harsh on dissenters and when these things are documented, we should reject overtures from those who rule such a country.

But the country I'm describing is not Chile—it is *Panama*.

We are negotiating with a dictatorship that comes within the portion of that map colored black for no freedom. No civil rights. One man rule. No free press.

Candidate Carter said he would never, relinquish "actual control" of the Panama Canal. President Carter is negotiating with a dictatorship whose record on civil and human rights is as I have just described and the negotiations concern the rights guaranteed to us by treaty which we will give up under a threat of violence. In only a few weeks we will mark the second anniversary of the death of freedom for the Vietnamese. An estimated 300,000 of them are being "re-educated" in concentration camps to forget about freedom.

There is only one major question on the agenda of national priorities and that is the state of our national security. I refer, of course, to the state of our armed forces—but also to our state of mind, to the way we perceive the world. We cannot maintain the strength we need to survive, no matter how many missiles we have, no matter how many tanks we build, unless we are willing to reverse:

—the trend of deteriorating faith in and continuing abuse of our national intelligence agencies. Let's stop the sniping and the propaganda and the historical revisionism and let the CIA and the other intelligence agencies do their job!

—Let us reverse the trend of public indifference to problems of national security. In every Congressional district citizens should join together, enlist and educate neighbors and make certain that Congressmen know we care. The front pages of major newspapers on the east coast recently headlined and told in great detail of a takeover, the takeover of a magazine published in New York—not a nation losing its

35

freedom. You would think, from the attention it received in the media, that it was a matter of blazing national interest whether the magazine lived or died. The tendency of much of the media to ignore the state of our national security is too well documented for me to go on.

My friends, the time has come to start acting to bring about the great conservative majority party we know is waiting to be created.

And just to set the record straight, let me say this about our friends who are now Republicans but who do not identify themselves as conservatives:

I want the record to show that I do not view the new revitalized Republican Party as one based on a principle of exclusion. After all, you do not get to be a majority party by searching for groups you *won't* associate or work with. If we truly believe in our principles, we should sit down and talk. Talk with anyone, anywhere, at any time if it means talking about the principles for the Republican Party. Conservatism is not a narrow ideology, nor is it the exclusive property of conservative activists.

We've succeeded better than we know. Little more than a decade ago more than two-thirds of Americans believed the federal government could solve all our problems, and do so withour restricting our freedom or bankrupting the Nation.

We warned of things to come; of the danger inherent in unwarranted government involvement in things not its proper province. What we warned against has come to pass. And today more than two-thirds of our citizens are telling us, and each other, that social engineering by the Federal government has failed. The Great Society is great only in power, in size and in cost. And so are the problems it set out to solve. Freedom has been diminished and we stand on the brink of economic ruin.

Our task now is not to sell a philosophy, but to make the majority of Americans, who already share that philosohy, see that modern conservatism offers them a political home. We are not a cult, we are members of a majority. Let's act and talk like it.

The job is ours and the job must be done. If not by us, who? if not now, when?

Our party must be the party of the individual. It must not sell out the individual to cater to the group. No greater challenge faces our society today than ensuring that each one of us can maintain his dignity and his identity in an increasingly complex, centralized society.

Extreme taxation, excessive controls, oppressive government competition with business, galloping inflation, frustrated minorities and forgotten Americans are not the products of free enterprise. They are the residue of centralized bureaucracy, of government by a self-anointed elite.

Our party must be based on the kind of leadership that grows and takes its strength from the people. Any organization is in actuality only the lengthened shadow of its members. A political party is a mechanical structure created to further a cause. The cause, not the mechanism, brings and holds the members together. And our cause must be to rediscover, reassert and reapply America's spiritual heritage to our national affairs.

Then with God's help we shall indeed be as a city upon a hill with the eyes of all people upon us.

IV

America's Purpose in the World

MARCH 17, 1978

This address was given approximately a year after President Carter took office and it gave Governor Reagan an opportunity to reflect on the still-new regime. Not surprisingly, he examined the record and found it wanting. This speech focused on the new President's foreign policy program, with particular attention to the controversial Panama Canal Treaty that Mr. Carter had negotiated.

As a part-time journalist faced with producing a syndicated daily radio broadcast and twice-a-week newspaper column, I find being on the mailing lists of an almost endless array of organizations most helpful. Now some of the flood of materials crosses my desk very swiftly. But not all of it. One thick handout I got late last year was especially fascinating, not only because of content but just because it was mailed to me at all.

It was from the White House Press Office. Under the title "Domestic and Foreign Policy Accomplishments" it told me, in 21 single-spaced pages, of the wonders of the Carter Administration's first year.

Beginning with the modest statement that—quote— "The President tackled directly and comprehensively major domestic problems that had been almost completely ignored in previous years."—unquote—it then recited an impressive list of major accomplishments. True, the White House hadn't claimed to find a way to control the weather or to eliminate crab grass on the White House lawn, but it did think it had solved— or nearly solved — our energy problems, Social Security's $17 trillion deficit, the size of a big government (we added 52,000 new employees in the first 10 months of 1977), the welfare mess and a host of other problems that have been center stage in American life for quite some time.

Tonight, perhaps we should discuss some of those White House claims and see if they have stood the test of even the three months that have passed since they were made. I know that's a little cruel—like checking up on someone's New Year's resolutions. After all, the Administration has scarcely gotten a single domestic program worth noting through Congress. I'll tell you what. Let us concentrate on the Administration's handling of foreign affairs, national security and its sense of priorities.

On priorities, there is the matter of issuing the former budget director a diplomatic passport; the taking of depositions from bartenders and issuing a 33-page denial that the President's chief aide expectorated at or in the direction of a young woman. It boggles the mind to think what they would have done if he'd spit on the sidewalk. Then there was the solemn oath to appoint and retain a U.S. attorney who goes investigating suspected wrongdoing on the part of Congressmen who belong to the President's own party.

Moving on to the Carter Administration's record in foreign affairs—let me say a few words about Panama and our canal there. And I do mean a few words.

With yesterday's vote on the so-called Neutrality treaty, you might say that Round One is over. Now, there has been confusion in some news reports which called this the "first treaty," saying that the Senate would next take up the "second" treaty. Actually, the Senate decided to reverse the procedure. The Neutrality treaty is the second treaty. They just voted on it first. Next they will deal with the basic treaty, the one called *the* Panama Canal treaty. It is the basic treaty because it is the one which would relinquish our rights and would actually eliminate the Canal Zone as soon as it goes into effect — if it does.

39

I hope the Senate will devote as much detailed attention to this basic treaty as it did to the Neutrality treaty. Meanwhile, I can't get a question out of my head. It is this: even though the Neutrality treaty supposedly guarantees our right to go back in to defend the Canal after 1999, if there is no Canal Zone, wouldn't any such move on out part be branded as interference in the internal affairs of Panama?

On the other hand, if the basic treaty is not ratified, the Neutrality treaty itself won't have much meaning because our rights and our presence in the Canal Zone would continue. And, when all is said and done, it is always easier to defend something you have than to get back something you gave away.

My fundamental concern has always been primarily with this basic treaty which would eliminate our rights there. I think there are alternatives to it which would be better for all concerned.

You are all activists, and I know you will make your views known to your elected representatives on this next treaty debate.

My purpose tonight, however, is not to repeat my views on this question. Panama *is* an important issue. The final outcome is not yet certain, and certainly the matter won't end with the final vote in the Senate. In a way, that will only begin it.

But, whatever the outcome on Capitol Hill, the smug assumptions of many of the treaties' proponents have been successfully and vigorously challenged.

Few Americans accept the belief of some of those now in positions of importance in guiding our foreign policy that America's purpose in the world is to appease the might out of a sense of fear or to appease the weak out of a sense of guilt.

But a question remains. Is the faulty thinking that has led us to these particular treaties an isolated particle, or is it part of a much larger whole?

In reviewing the foreign policy of this Administration, one can only come to the conclusion that the mistaken assumptions that led to its course on the Panama Canal treaties are being duplicated around the world.

Its policy is rooted in well-meaning intentions, but it shows a woeful uncertainty as to America's purpose in the world.

The Administration *means* to do good by espousing a human rights doctrine it cannot define, much less implement. In the process, this policy has met with scorn from our enemies and alarm from our friends. That self-graded 21-page White House report card said, with regard to human rights, "The President has strengthened our human rights policy and we are letting it be known clearly that the United States stands with the victims of repression." Is that why our representatives at the Belgrade Conference remained silent in the face of a final report that contained not one word about Russian violations of the human rights provisions in the Helsinki Agreement?

If the Carter Administration "stand with the victims of repression," the people of Cuba, Panama, Vietnam, Cambodia, and the mainland of China have yet to hear about it. The fact is, the Carter human rights policy is whatever his appointees who guide it want it to be. In practice, they have ceaselessly scolded authoritarian governments of countries that are friendly and ignored authoritarian and totalitarian countries that are not.

Mr. Carter might find a reading of the historian Charles Beard informative. Nearly 40 years ago, Beard concluded that the defect of a foreign policy based on what he called "the selfish sacrifice required by an absolute morality" was the inability to understand "the limited nature of American powers to relieve, restore and maintain life beyond its own sphere of interest and control—a recognition of the hard fact that the United States . . . did not possess the power . . . to assure the establishment of democratic and pacific government."

But, by using a combination of heavy-handed moves against allied countries, on the one hand, and making "pre-emptive concessions" toward unfriendly or potentially unfriendly countries on the other, the Carter Administration has managed to convey the view that it desperately wants the whole world to have democratic institutions that would be the envy of the most ardent ACLU lawyer, and that wishing will make it so.

That view of the world ranks along with belief in the Tooth

41

Fairy. But confusion of purpose and a false sense of guilt are not the only elements in this Administration's foreign policy.

Too often, the President is advised by men and women who are forever trapped in the tragic but still fresh memory of a lost war. And from Vietnam they have drawn all the wrong lessons.

When they say "never again," they mean the United States should never again resist communist aggression.

In saying "never again," implying that the war *should* have been lost; that it is all right for the victors to conduct a brutal campaign against their own people, violating even minimal human rights.

That it is alright to ignore these massive violations and alright for us to seek better relations with the governments responsible. That White House document lists as an "accomplishment" the fact that "the Administration has started the process of normalizing relations" with the communist conquerors of South Vietnam. The lesson we should have learned from Vietnam is that never again will Americans be asked to fight and die unless they are permitted to win.

We need a foreign policy stripped of platitudes, cant and mere moral earnestness—an earnestness fatally compromised by the massive crimes of some of the communist world's newer members.

This pattern of Communist violations of human rights should come as no surprise to us. Over and over again, newly established Marxist regimes have committed them. In the 1920's and '30s it was the Soviet Union; in the late '40s the new Iron Curtain countries; in the '50s and through the Cultural Revolution of the '60s it was Communist China and Cuba; and now it is Vietnam and Cambodia.

The problem with much of the Carter team is that they know too little, not too much of history. And, they have lost faith in their own country's past and traditions.

Too often, that team has operated under the assumption that the United States must prove and reprove and prove again its goodness to the world. Proving that we are civilized in a world that is often uncivilized—and unapologetically so—is hardly necessary.

42

The themes of a sound foreign policy should be no mystery, nor the result of endless agonizing reappraisals. They are rooted in our past; in our very beginning as a nation.

The founding fathers established a system which meant a radical break from that which preceded it. A written constitution would provide a permanent form of government, limited in scope, but effective in providing both liberty and order.

Government was not to be a matter of self-appointed rulers, governing by whim or harsh ideology. It was not to be government *by* the strongest or *for* the few.

Our principles were revolutionary. We began as a small, weak republic. But we survived. Our example inspired others, imperfectly at times, but it inspired them nevertheless.

This constitutional republic, conceived in liberty and dedicated to the proposition that all men are created equal, prospered and grew strong.

To this day, America is still the abiding alternative to tyranny. That is our purpose in the world—nothing more and nothing less.

To carry out that purpose our fundamental aim in foreign policy must be to ensure our own survival and to protect those others who share our values.

Under no circumstances should we have any illusions about the intentions of those who are enemies of freedom. Our communist adversaries have little regard for human rights because they have little interest in human freedom. The ruling elites of those countries wish only one thing: to preserve their privileges and to eliminate the nagging reminder that others have done and are doing better under freedom.

Every American President since World War II has known or quickly learned that the Soviet Union, for example, is not benign in its intentions.

The Soviet Union has no interest in maintaining the status quo. It does not accept our soft definition of "detente." To the Soviet Union, "detente" is an opportunity to expand its sphere of influence around the world.

The Soviet Union has steadily increased its capacity for such expansion. That capability has grown enormously since 1945 and, above all, since 1962 when the Cold War was first declared "over" by the hopeful and naive.

Today, the USSR continues its drive to dominate the world in military capability: on land, on water, and in the air. Meanwhile, the Carter Administration seems confused and torn, partly believing the realities and partly listening to those who believe that pre-emptive concession by the Soviets. But they don't bargain that way. They understand strength; they exploit weakness and take advantage of inexperience. And, possibly, it was inexperience that led the President to placate the most dovish members of his party by scuttling the B-1 bomber—one of his bargaining chips—even before the SALT II negotiations began.

One of the reasons given for cancellation of the B-1 was economy, and even here there was a lack of accuracy. First of all, the price given for the aircraft was what the price will be in 1986 if inflation continues—which incidentally suggests a lack of resolve in the Administration's anti-inflation fight. Second, we were told the B-52 or the F-111 could be modified to do the job the B-1 was supposed to do. Here the cost differential shrinks sizeably when we look at the facts. The modification itself is quite costly, and we can double that cost. It will take two planes to substitute for every B-1 because the B-1 carries twice the payload the others will. It will carry that load twice as fast in a plane only half the size of a B-52, and it is far less vulnerable to the Soviet defense system.

While confusion and conflicting advice seem to tug and pull at the White House, the Soviet Union continues to build up its capability for world domination. It has even gone so far as to put entire factories underground and to disperse much of its industrial capacity — the most sophisticated civil defense program ever developed. The knowledge that our strategic missiles, if they ever *had* to be used, would inflict minimal damage on the Soviets, compared to the havoc theirs would produce on our continent, should, in itself, be sufficient to spur the Administration to making certain that we be No. 1 in the world in terms of national defense capabilities. So far, though, this does not seem to be a White House priority.

44

Today, we can see the brunt of the Soviet Union's capabilities at work in the Horn of Africa.

To most Americans, that part of the world seems remote, as Korea and Vietnam seemed remote, along with those other places where the Soviets have sought advantage.

In Ethiopia, formerly a close friend of the United States, the Soviets with their Cuban foreign legion have turned that country into a Free Fire Zone in order to subdue Ethiopia's two principal enemies, Somalia and the Eritrean rebels.

The Soviet goal is obvious: to secure a permanent foothold for itself on the Red Sea.

If the Soviets are successful—and it looks more and more as if they will be—then the entire Horn of Africa will be under their influence, if not their control. From there, they can threaten the sea lanes carrying oil to western Europe and the United States, if and when they choose.

More immediately, control of the Horn of Africa would give Moscow the ability to destabilize those governments on the Arabian peninsula which have proven themselves strongly anti-communist. Among them are some of the world's principal oil exporters.

Moscow can also turn its full attention south if it can ensure its position in the Horn of Africa. It takes no great stretch of the imagination to see that Rhodesia is a tempting target. Cuban leaders now boast that it is.

What are we doing about it? Apparently, our response to the Rhodesian settlement proposed by the moderate black leaders and Prime Minister Ian Smith is not to tell the Soviets—behind the scenes — to get lost or risk pressures elsewhere that they won't like. No, our response seems to be best summed up by our ambassador to the United Nations, who is unhappy with the moderate, democratic solution in Rhodesia because he's afraid (he says) it will bring on a massive Soviet arms buildup. What does he think we're having now?

He seems to believe that the only Rhodesian plan we can afford to support is one to the liking of the two terrorist guerrilla leaders. But if they have their way, one or the other of them will become the sole power in Rhodesia, fronting of course for the

45

Soviet Union. Unless we want to make the world safe for terrorist guerrillas, the only sensible course is for us to support the moderate solution in Rhodesia and quietly tell Moscow to keep its hands off — unless, of course, we are too weak to do that. Is *that* what Mr. Young is trying to tell us? I hope not, for a Marxist Rhodesia would lead to even *more* tempting targets for Moscow in Africa. Perhaps Djibouti, Sudan, Chad, the old Spanish Sahara (where guerrillas are already in operation).

And one other which will cost us dearly. Whatever we may think of South Africa's internal policies, control of its mineral riches and its strategic position are the Soviet Union's ultimate goal in Africa.

Unless the White House can bring itself to understand these realities, it is not too much to say that in a few years we may be faced with the prospect of a Soviet empire of proteges and dependencies stretching from Addis Ababa to Capetown. Those who now reject that possibility out of hand — and they seem to have the ear of the man in the Oval Office — have yet to explain Angola, Mozambique, the situation in the Horn of Africa or the terrorists in Rhodesia.

One thing is certain: Soviet successes will not breed caution in the Kremlin. Rather, the reverse.

Those in the Carter Administration who are not even inclined to protest the recent Soviet moves assure us that, sooner or later, the Soviets will make serious mistakes and our doing nothing will hasten that day.

But to say, as they do, that all is well because the Soviets are creating their own Vietnam is nonsense. These Carter advisers seem to forget that the Soviets won in Vietnam and they intend to win again—this time in Africa. They learned the *true* lesson of the Vietnam war: certainty of purpose and ruthlessness of execution wins wars. Vietnam held no terror for the Soviets as it did for so many Americans. And, adventures in Africa hold no terror for them either.

To say, as some in the Administration do, that African nationalism will stop the Soviets is the weakest reed of all. The reason is simple: African nationalism, as such, does not exist. No African government has yet condemned the Russians, nor

46

do the halls of the Organization of African Unity ring with anti-Soviet slogans — perhaps because those halls happen to be in Addis Ababa, the capital of Ethiopia.

The criticism by African states of the Soviets that the Administration seems to be so desperately hoping for will not materialize. After all, there is in Africa, as around the world, a healthy respect for power and the determined use of power.

One veteran West European diplomat put the African situation in perspective recently. He was quoted as saying, "This situation is going to make the leaders of a lot of these small, weak nations stop and think. And what do they see on the American side? Apparent indecision, attempts to talk, a reluctance to give weapons to friends"—and, he might have added: a "belief that there are nasty, immoral wars of imperialist aggression and nice clean wars of national liberation."

The Administration's uncertainty of purpose isn't confined to the world's current hot spots. It is apparent even in our own hemisphere.

That White House tally sheet I mentioned listed its "accomplishments" in Latin America. It said, "The Administration has developed a new global approach to Latin America. . . ."

Well, what it *has* done from the beginning was to accept the notions fashionable in the most liberal circles that surrender of the Panama Canal and *rapprochement* with Cuba were the keys to successful relations with Latin America.

Nothing could have been further from the truth. Of Panama, I have already had a good deal to say. But let me say again, we have earned no respect or lasting affection in Latin America with *these* treaties.

Unfortunately, our policy toward Latin America has not only entailed friendship for one dictator who is a sworn enemy and for another who routinely suppresses human rights and may be involved in the worst sort of corruption — that policy has also entailed hostility toward our friends.

Let me cite just one example, Brazil. An ally in World War II, (contributing a division which saw hard action in Europe), a friend through most of the '60s and now a great hope for con-

47

tributing to the future industrial strength of the West, Brazil now finds itself turned on by us — with a vengeance. Whatever the motives, human rights or worries over nuclear proliferation, the ends did not justify the means. The result is that we have nearly lost a friend without achieving any of the Administration's professed objectives.

It is time to try another approach, an approach based on reality and not the slogans and romantic notions of ideologues who just happen to have access to the Oval Office.

First, let us end this cycle of American indifference, followed by frenzied activity in Latin America (as it has been elsewhere). It leaves our southern neighbors bewildered and cynical. Instead, I propose a steadier course in which Latin America's growing importance is recognized not as an act of charity, but in our own self-interest.

Latin America, with all its resources and vitality, should be encouraged to join not the Third World, much less the communists' Second World, but the First World—that community of stable, prosperous and free nations of Western Europe, North America and Japan.

Today, there is hope that much of Latin America might do so. First, many nations have learned the cost of Socialist experimentation. Argentina under the Perons. Chile under Allende. Peru under Velasco, Mexico under Echeverria. All suffered economic catastrophe. Their successors learned the bitter truth that defying the laws of economics benefits no one and, in fact, hurts most the poor whose cause those earlier leaders so demagogically espoused.

Today, as a result of those experiments which went so badly out of control, more and more of our neighbors are turning to the free market as a model of development. Their acceptance of economic rationality should be neither ignored nor penalized, but actively encouraged.

At the same time, we must recognize that Latin America is once again leaving a period of strictly military rule and entering a more democratic phase. But in this case, the United States is doing too much pushing, rather than too little.

Unhappily, the change from military to civilian rule is not an easy one. Nor can it be rushed. If it is, we will only succeed in creating weak and vulnerable democratic governments that will soon be swept out of power by just another generation of military strongmen even more convinced of the defects of democracy.

Above all, we want a free and prosperous Latin America. And, to obtain that, we cannot continue to reward our self-declared enemies and then turn around and punish our friends.

That leads me again to Panama. The treaties that have occupied so much of our attention in recent months represent both the good instincts and the bad impulses of American diplomacy.

The bad, for reasons I have repeated on many occasions: the feeling that we are guilty of some sin for which we must now atone; and our inability to say "no," not out of truculence, but because it was the proper thing to say to secure our interests and to reaffirm our greater responsibility, which is leadership of all that remains of the free world.

Yes, the treaties represent the good instincts of American diplomacy, too; a spirit of generosity and willingness to change with times. A good foreign policy must have both elements—the need to say "no" and the willingness to change—in just the right proportions. Unfortunately, accepting change because it seems fashionable to do so, with little real regard for the consequences, seems to dominate our foreign policy today.

Too many in positions of importance believe that through generosity and self-effacement we can avoid trouble, whether it's with Panama and the Canal or the Soviet Union and SALT.

But, like it or not, trouble will not be avoided. The American people and their elected leaders will continue to be faced with hard choices and difficult moments, for resolve is continually being tested by those who envy us our prosperity and begrudge us our freedom.

America will remain great and act responsibly so long as it exercises power—wisely, and not in the bullying sense—but exercises it, nonetheless.

Leadership is a great burden. We grow weary of it at times.

And the Carter Administration, despite its own cheerful propaganda about accomplishments, reflects that weariness.

But if *we* are not to shoulder the burdens of leadership in the free world, then who will?

The alternatives are neither pleasant nor acceptable. Great nations which fail to meet their responsibilities are consigned to the dustbin of history. We grew from that small, weak republic which had as its assets spirit, optimism, faith in God and an unshakeable belief that free men and women could govern themselves wisely. We became the leader of the free world, an example for all those who cherish freedom.

If we are to continue to be that example—if we are to preserve our own freedom—we must understand those who would dominate us and deal with them with determination.

We must shoulder our burden with our eyes fixed on the future, but recognizing the realities of today, not counting on mere hope or wishes. We must be willing to carry out our responsibility as the custodian of individual freedom. Then we will achieve our destiny to be as a shining city on a hill for all mankind to see.

V

Our Time is Now. Our Moment Has Arrived.

MARCH 20, 1981

The 1981 "Reagan Banquet," as the Governor's annual CPAC addresses had come to be known, was a memorable, triumphal and emotional evening because it wasn't "Governor" Reagan who was speaking, but rather, "President" Reagan.

The setting—the Mayflower Hotel Ball Room — was familiar, but it was obvious that a dramatic change had occurred. At the reception, guests who in earlier years had jostled and joshed Governor Reagan now fell silent and respectful in the presence of "the President."

The man who in earlier years had arrived accompanied only by Mrs. Reagan and one or two aides now arrived in a motorcade accompanied by a phalanx of advancemen, security personnel and assistants of all types.

Outside, the staff of the hotel had assembled to greet him, and across the street police were holding back a noisy crowd of picketers.

When the President and First Lady entered the Ballroom they did so not to the strains of "California Here I Come" as in years past but to "Ruffles and Flourishes" and "Hail to the Chief."

Following one of the most emotional receptions ever accorded him, the new President responded with one of the most poetic and moving addresses of his public life.

Addressing the conservative activists, he told them their years in the political wilderness were over; that his victory was "your victory."

51

Saluting the activists who had stood by him, he summoned them to the task of enacting the conservative agenda into law.

M R. CHAIRMAN AND CONGRESSMAN MICKEY EDWARDS, thank you very much. My goodness, I can't realize how much time has gone by, because I remember when I first knew Mickey, he was just a clean-shaved boy. But thank you for inviting me here once again. And as Mickey told you, with the exception of those two years, it is true about how often I've been here. So, let me say now that I hope we'll be able to keep this tradition going forward and that you'll invite me again next year.

And in the rough days ahead, and I know there will be such days, I hope that you'll be like the mother of the young lad in camp when the camp director told her that he was going to have to discipline her son. And she said, "Well, don't be too hard on him. He's very sensitive. Slap the boy next to him, and that will scare Irving." But let us also, tonight, salute those with vision who labored to found this group—the American Conservative Union, the Young Americans for Freedom, *National Review* and *Human Events*.

It's been said that anyone who seeks success or greatness should first forget about both and seek only the truth, and the rest will follow. Well, fellow truthseekers, none of us here tonight—contemplating the seal on this podium and a balanced budget in 1984—can argue with that kind of logic. For whatever history does finally say about our cause, it must say: The conservative movement in 20th century America held fast through hard and difficult years to its vision of the truth. And history must also say that our victory, when it was achieved, was not so much a victory of politics as it was a victory of ideas, not so much a victory for any one man or party as it was a victory for a set of principles—principles that were protected and nourished by a few unselfish Americans through many grim and heartbreaking defeats.

Now, you are those Americans that I'm talking about. I

52

wanted to be here not just to acknowledge your efforts on my behalf, not just to remark that last November's victory was singularly your victory, not just to mention that the new administration in Washington is a testimony to your perseverance and devotion to principle, but to say, simply "Thank you," and to say those words not as a President, or even as a conservative; thank you as an American. I say this knowing that there are many in this room whose talents might have entitled them to a life of affluence but who chose another career out of a higher sense of duty to country. And I know, too, that the story of their selflessness will never be written up in *Time* or *Newsweek* or go down in the history books.

You know, on an occasion like this it's a little hard not to reminisce, not to think back and just realize how far we've come. The Portuguese have a word for such recollection—*saudade*—a poetic term rich with the dreams of yesterday. And surely in our past there was many a dream littered with broken lances.

Who can forget that July night in San Francisco when Barry Goldwater told us that we must set the tides running again in the cause of freedom, and he said, "until our cause has won the day, inspired the world, and shown the way to a tomorrow worthy of all our yesteryears?" And had there not been a Barry Goldwater willing to take the lonely walk, we wouldn't be here talking of a celebration tonight.

But our memories are not just political ones. I like to think back about a small, artfully written magazine named *National Review*, founded in 1955 and ridiculed by the intellectual establishment because it published an editorial that said it would stand athwart the course of history yelling, "Stop!" And then there was a spritely written newsweekly coming out of Washington named *Human Events* that many said would never be taken seriously, but it would become later "must reading" not only for Capitol Hill insiders but for all of those in public life.

How many of us were there who used to go home from meetings like this with no thought of giving up, but still find ourselves wondering in the dark of night whether this much-loved land might go the way of other great nations that lost a sense of mission and a passion for freedom?

There are so many people and institutions who come to mind for their role in the success we celebrate tonight. Intellectual leaders like Russel Kirk, Friedrich Hayek, Henry Hazlitt, Milton Friedman, James Burnham, Ludwig von Mises — they shaped so much of our thoughts.

It's especially hard to believe that it was only a decade ago, on a cold April day on a small hill in upstate New York, that another of these great thinkers, Frank Meyer, was buried. He'd made the awful journey that so many others had: he pulled himself from the clutches of "The God That Failed," and then in his writing fashioned a vigorous new synthesis of tradition and libertarian thought — a synthesis that is today recognized by many as modern conservatism.

It was Frank Meyer who reminded us that the robust individualism of the American experience was part of the deeper current of Western learning and culture. He pointed out that a respect for law, an appreciation for tradition, and regard for the social consensus that gives stability to our public and private institutions, these civilized ideas must still motivate us even as we seek a new economic prosperity based on reducing government interference in the marketplace.

Our goals complement each other. We're not cutting the budget simply for the sake of sounder financial management. This is only a first step toward returning power to the States and communities, only a first step toward reordering the relationship between citizen and government. We can make government again responsive to the people by cutting its size and scope and thereby ensuring that its legitimate functions are performed efficiently and justly.

Because ours is a consistent philosophy of government, we can be very clear: We do not have a separate social agenda, a separate economic agenda, and a separate foreign agenda. We have one agenda. Just as surely as we seek to put our financial house in order and rebuild our nation's defenses, so too we seek to protect the unborn, to end the manipulation of schoolchildren by utopian planners, and permit the acknowledgement of a Supreme Being in our classrooms, just as we allow such acknowledgements in other public institutions.

54

Now, obviously we're not going to be able to accomplish all this at once. The American people are patient. I think they realize that the wrongs done over several decades cannot be corrected instantly. You know, I had the pleasure in appearing before a Senate committee once while I was still Governor, and I was challenged because there was a Republican President in the White House who'd been there for several months — why we hadn't corrected everything that had been done. And the only way I could think to answer him was I told him about a ranch many years ago that Nancy and I acquired. It had a barn with eight stalls in it in which they kept cattle, and we wanted to keep horses. And I was in there day after day with a pick and a shovel, lowering the level of those stalls, which had accumulated over the years. And I told this Senator who'd asked that question that I discovered that you did not undo in weeks or months what it had taken some 15 years to accumulate.

I also believe that we conservatives, if we mean to continue governing, must realize that it will not be so easy to place the blame on the past for our national difficulties. You know, one day the great baseball manager Frankie Frisch sent a rookie out to play center field. The rookie promptly dropped the first fly ball that was hit to him. On the next play he let a grounder go between his feet and then threw the ball to the wrong base. Frankie stormed out of the dugout, took his glove away from him and said, "I'll show you how to play this position." And the next batter slammed a line drive right over second base. Frankie came on it, missed it completely, fell down when he tried to chase it, threw down his glove, and yelled at the rookie, "You've got the center field so screwed up nobody can play it."

The point is we must lead a nation, and that means more than criticizing the past. Indeed, as T. S. Eliot once said, "Only by acceptance of the past will you alter its meaning."

Now, during our political efforts, we were the subject of much indifference and oftentimes intolerance, and that's why I hope our political victory will be remembered as a generous one and our time in power will be recalled for the tolerance we showed for those with whom we disagree.

But beyond this, beyond this we have to offer America and

the world a larger vision. We must remove government's smothering hand from where it does harm; we must seek to revitalize the proper function of government. But we do these things to set loose again the energy and the ingenuity of the American people. We do these things to reinvigorate those social and economic institutions which serve as a buffer and a bridge between the individual and the state—and which remain the real source of our progress as a people.

And we must hold out this exciting prospect of an orderly, compassionate, pluralistic society—an archipelago of prospering communities and divergent institutions—a place where a free and energetic people can work out their own destiny under God.

I know that some will think about the perilous world we live in and the dangerous decade before us and ask what practical effect this conservative vision can have today. When Prime Minister Thatcher was here recently we both remarked on the sudden, overwhelming changes that had come recently to politics in both our countries.

At our last official function, I told the Prime Minister that everywhere we look in the world the cult of the state is dying. And I held out hope that it wouldn't be long before those of our adversaries who preach the supremacy of the state were remembered only for their role in a sad, rather bizarre chapter in human history. The largest planned economy in the world has to buy food elsewhere or its people would starve.

We've heard in our century far too much of the sounds of anguish from those who live under totalitarian rule. We've seen too many monuments made not out of marble or stone but out of barbed wire and terror.

But from these terrible places have come survivors, witnesses to the triumph of the human spirit over the mystique of state power, prisoners whose spiritual values made them the rulers of their guards. With their survival, they brought us ''the secret of the camps,'' a lesson for our time and for any age: Evil is powerless if the good are unafraid.

That's why the Marxist vision of man without God must eventually be seen as an empty and a false faith—the second oldest in the world—proclaimed in the Garden of Eden with whispered words of temptation: "Ye shall be as gods." The crisis of the Western world, Whittaker Chambers reminded us, exists to the degree in which it is indifferent to God. "The Western world does not know it," he said about our struggle, "but it already possesses the answer to this problem—but only provided that its faith in God and the freedom He enjoins is as great as communism's faith in man."

This is the real task before us: to reassert our commitment as a nation to a law higher than our own, to renew our own, to renew our spiritual strength. Only by building a wall of such spiritual resolve can we, as a free people, hope to protect our own heritage and make it someday the birthright of all men.

There is, in America, a greatness and a tremendous heritage of idealism which is a reservoir of strength and goodness. It is ours if we will but tap it. And, because of this—because that greatness is there—there is need in America today for a reaffirmation of that goodness and a reformation of our greatness.

The dialogue and the deeds of the past few decades are not sufficient to the day in which we live. They cannot keep the promise of tomorrow. The encrusted bureaucracies and the engrained procedures which have developed of late respond neither to the minority or the majority. We've come to a turning point. We have a decision to make. Will we continue with yesterday's agenda and yesterday's failures, or will we reassert our ideals and our standards, will we reaffirm our faith, and renew our purpose? This is a time for choosing.

I made a speech by that title in 1964. I said, "We've been told increasingly that we must choose between left or right." But we're still using those terms—left or right. And I'll repeat what I said then in '64. "There is no left or right. There's only an up or down": up to the ultimate in individual freedom, man's age old dream, the ultimate in individual freedom, consistent with an orderly society—or down to the totalitarianism of the ant heap. And those today who, however good their intentions, tell us that we should trade freedom for security are on that downward path.

Those of us who call ourselves conservative have pointed out what's wrong with government policy for more than a quarter of a century. Now we have an opportunity to make policy and to change our national direction. All of us in government—in the House, in the Senate, in the executive branch—and in private life can now stand together. We can stop the drain on the economy by the public sector. We can appoint to the bench distinguished judges who understand the first responsibility of any legal system is to punish the guilty and protect the innocent. We can restore to their rightful place in our national consciousness the values of family, work, neighborhood, and religion. And, finally, we can see to it that the nations of the world clearly understand America's intentions and respect for resolve.

Now we have the opportunity—yes, and the necessity—to prove that the American promise is equal to the task of redressing our grievances and equal to the challenge of inventing a great tomorrow.

This reformation, this renaissance will not be achieved nor will it be served by those who engage in political claptrap or false promises. It will not be achieved by those who set people against people, class against class, or institution against institution. So, while we celebrate our recent political victory we must understand there's much work before us: to gain control again of government, to reward personal initiative and risk-taking in the marketplace, to revitalize our system of federalism, to strengthen the private institutions that make up the independent sector of our society, and to make our own spiritual affirmation in the face of those who would deny man has a place before God. Not easy tasks perhaps. But I would remind you as I did on January 20th, they're not impossible, because, after all, we're Americans.

This year we will celebrate a victory won two centuries ago in Yorktown, the victory of a small, fledging nation over a mighty world power. How many people are aware—I've been told that a British band played the music at that surrender ceremony because we didn't have a band. [Laughter] And they played a tune that was very popular in England at the time. Its title was ''The World Turned Upside Down.'' I'm sure it was far more appropriate than they realized at that moment. The heritage

58

from that long difficult struggle is before our eyes today in this city, in the great halls of our government and in the monuments to the memory of our great men.

It is the heritage that evokes the images of a much-loved land, a land of struggling settlers and lonely immigrants, of giant cities and great frontiers, images of all that our country is and all that we want her to be. That's the America entrusted to us, to stand by, to protect, and yes, to lead her wisely.

Fellow citizens, fellow conservatives, our time is now. Our moment has arrived. We stand together shoulder to shoulder in the thickest of the fight. If we carry the day and turn the tide, we can hope that as long as men speak of freedom and those who have protected it, they will remember us, and they will say, ''Here were the brave and here their place of honor.''

VI

The Agenda Is Victory
February 26, 1982

President Reagan's 1982 CPAC address was made to an audience that included many members of the Cabinet and White House staff and to several hundred others sitting in an adjoining ballroom.

Much had happened since his last appearance. A would-be assassin's bullet had brought him close to death, his tax cut program had been enacted into law; his first round of domestic spending cuts had been passed and a large-scale defense buildup had begun.

The Reagan policy initiatives had all been effected over great opposition, and now that the country was in the first months of what would prove a very deep recession, the voices of the critics were getting louder.

Looking ahead to the fall midterm elections, President Reagan vowed to press ahead with his agenda, and he asked for help in maintaining conservative gains in Congress.

MR. TOASTMASTER [REPRESENTATIVE] MICKEY EDWARDS, thank you very much for those generous words — reverend clergy, ladies and gentlemen, we're delighted to be here at the ninth annual Conservative Political Action Conference.

Anyone looking at the exciting program you've scheduled over these four days, and the size of this gathering here tonight, can't help but be impressed with the energy and vitality of the conservative movement in America. We owe a special debt of gratitude to the staffs of American Conservative Union, Young Americans for Freedom, *Human Events* and *National Review*, for making this year's conference the most successful in the brief but impressive history of this event.

Now, you may remember that when I spoke to you last year, I said the election victory we enjoyed in November of 1980 was not a victory of politics so much as it was a victory of ideas; not a victory for any one man or party, but a victory for a set of principles, principles that had been protected and nourished during the years of grim and heartbreaking defeats by a few dedicated Americans. Well, you are those Americans, and I salute you.

I've also come here tonight to remind you of how much remains to be done, and to ask your help in turning into reality even more of our hopes for America and the world. The agenda for this conference is victory, victory in this year's crucial congressional, State, and local elections.

The media coverage that you've received this week, the attention paid to you by so many distinguished Americans in and out of government—conservative and not so conservative— are testimony to the sea-change that you've already brought about in American politics. But, despite the glitter of nights like this and the excitement we all still feel at the thought of enacting reforms we were only able to talk about a few years ago, we should always remember that our strength still lies in our faith in the good sense of the American people. And that the climate in Washington is still opposed to those enduring values, those "permanent things" that we've always believed in.

But Washington's fascination with passing trends and one-day headlines can sometimes cause serious problems over in the West Wing of the White House—they cause them. There's the problem of leaks. Before we even announced the giveaway of surplus cheese, the warehouse mice had hired a lobbyist. [Laughter] And then a few weeks ago, those stories broke about the Kennedy tapes. And that caused something of a stir. Al Haig came in to brief me on his trip to Europe. I uncapped my pen, and he stopped talking. [Laughter] Up on the hill, I understand they were saying, "You need eloquence in the State Dining

Room, wit in the East Room, and sign language in the Oval Office.'' [Laughter] It got so bad that I found myself telling every visitor there were absolutely no tape recordings being made. And if they wanted a transcript of that remark, just mention it to the potted plant on their way out. [Laughter]

But Washington is a place of fads and one-week stories. It's also a company town, and the company's name is government, big government. Now, I have a sneaking suspicion that a few of you might have agreed when we decided not to ask Congress for higher taxes. And I hope you realize it's going to take more than 402 days to completely change what's been going on for 40 years.

I realized that the other day when I read a story about a private citizen in Louisiana who asked the government for help in developing his property. And he got back a letter that said, ''We have observed that you have not traced the title prior to 1803. Before the final approval, it will be necessary that the title be traced previous to that year. Well, the citizen's answer was eloquent.

''Gentlemen,'' he wrote, ''I am unaware that any educated man failed to know that Louisiana was purchased from France in 1803. The title of the land was acquired by France by the right of conquest from Spain. The land came in the possession of Spain in 1492 by the discovery by an Italian sailor, Christopher Columbus. The good Queen Isabella took the precaution of recieving the blessing of the Pope. . . . The Pope is emissary of the Son of God, who made the world. Therefore, I believe that it is safe to assume that He also made that part of the United States called Louisiana. And I hope to hell you're satisfied.'' [Laughter]

Now, changing the habits of four decades is, as I say, going to take more than 402 days. But change will come if we conservatives are in this for the long haul, if we owe our first loyalty to the ideas and principles we discussed, debated, developed, and popularized over the years. Last year I pointed to these principles as the real source of our strength as a political movement, and mentioned some of the intellectual giants who fostered and developed them—men like Frank Meyer, who reminded us that

62

the robust individualism of America was part of deeper currents in Western civilization, currents that dictated respect for the law and the careful preservation of our political traditions.

Only a short time ago, conservatives filled this very room for a testimonial dinner to a great conservative intellect and scholar, author of the "The Conservative Mind," Russell Kirk. In a recent speech, Dr. Kirk has offered some political advice for the upcoming elections. He said now, more than ever, we must seek out the "gift of audacity." We must not become too comfortable with our new-found status in Washington. "When the walls of order are breached, the vigorous conservative must exlaim: Arm me, audacity, from head to foot." It was Napoleon, master of the huge battalions, who once said, "It is imagination that rules the human races." And Disraeli who mentioned that "success is the child of audacity."

We must approach the upcoming elections with a forthright and direct message for the American people. We must remind them of the economic catastrophe that we faced on January 20th, 1981: millions out of work, inflation in double digits for two years in a row, interest rates hovering at 21½ per cent, productivity and the rate of growth in the gross national product down for the third year in a row, the money supply increasing by 12 per cent—and all this due to one overriding cause: Government was too big and had spent too much money.

Federal spending, in the last decade, went up more than 300 per cent. In 1980 alone, it increased by 17 per cent. Almost three-quarters of the Federal budget was routinely referred to as "uncontrollable," largely due to increases in programs like food stamps, which in 15 years had increased by 16,000 per cent, or Medicare and Medicaid—up by more than 500 per cent in just 10 years. Our national debt was approaching $1 trillion, and we were paying nearly $100 billion a year in interest on that debt— more than enough money to run the Federal Government only 20 years ago.

In an effort to keep pace, taxes had increased by 220 per cent in just 10 years, and we were looking at a tax increase from 1980 to 1984, already passed before we got here, of more than $300 billion. Unless we stop the spending juggernaut and reverse the trend toward even higher taxes, government by 1984 would be taking nearly one-quarter of the gross national product. Inflation and interest rates, according to several studies, would be heading toward 25 per cent—levels that would stifle enterprise and initiative and plunge the Nation into even deeper economic crisis.

At this point last year, much of the smart money in Washington was betting, as it is today, on the failure of our proposals for restoring the economy, that we could never assemble the votes we needed to get our program for economic recovery through the Congress. But assemble the votes we did. For the first time in nearly 25 years, we slowed the spending juggernaut and got the taxpayers out from under the Federal steamroller. We cut the rate of growth in Federal spending almost in half. We lowered inflation to a single-digit rate, and it's still going down. It was 8.9 per cent for all of 1981, but our January figure, at an annualized rate, is only 3½ per cent.

When they talk of what should be done for the poor, well, one thing alone, by reducing inflation, we increased the purchasing power of poor families by more than $250. We cut taxes for business and individuals and index to inflation. This last step ended once and for all that hidden profit on inflation that had made the Federal bureaucracy America's largest growth industry.

We've moved against waste and fraud with a task force including our Inspectors General, who have already found thousands of people who've been dead for as long as seven years still receiving benefit checks from the government. We've concentrated on criminal prosecutions, and we've cut back in other areas like the multitude of films, pamphlets, and public relations experts, or, as we sometimes call them, the Federal flood of flicks and flacks and foldouts.

We're cutting the size of the Federal payroll by 75,000 over the next few years and are fighting to dismantle the Department of Energy and the Department of Education, agencies whose policies have frequently been exactly the opposite of what we need for real energy growth and sound education for our children.

Even now, less than five months after our program took full effect, we've seen the first signs of recovery. In January, leading economic indicators like housing permits showed an upturn. By 1983 we will begin bringing down the percentage of the gross national produce consumed by both the Federal deficit and by Federal spending and taxes.

Our situation now is in some ways similar to that which confronted the United States and other Western nations shortly after World War II. Many economists then were predicting a return to depression once the stimulus of wartime spending was ended. But people were weary of wartime goverment controls, and here and in other nations like West Germany those controls were eliminated against the advice of some experts. At first, there was a period of hardship—higher unemployment and declining growth. In fact, in 1946, our gross national product dropped 15 percent, but by 1947, the next year, it was holding steady and in 1948 increased by four per cent. Unemployment began a steady decline. And in 1949 consumer prices were decreasing. A lot of the experts underestimated the economic growth that occurs once government stops meddling and the people take over. Well, they were wrong then, and they're wrong now.

The job of this administration and of the Congress is to move forward with additional cuts in the growth of Federal spending and thereby ensure America's economic recovery. We have proposed budget cuts for 1983, and our proposals have met with cries of anguish. And those who utter the cries are equally anguished because there will be a budget deficit. They're a little like a dog sitting on a sharp rock howling with pain, when all he has to do is get up and move.

On the spending cuts now before the Congress and those tax reductions we've already passed for the American people, let me state we're standing by our program. We will not turn back or sound retreat.

You know, if I could just interject here, some of those people who say we must change direction when we've only been on this new direction for five months—and it's only the first limited phase of the whole program—it was described pretty well by

Mickey Edwards, sitting right here, while we were having dinner. He said, ''If you were sliding downhill on a snowy hill, and you know there's a cliff down there ahead of you at the bottom and suddenly there's a road that turns off at to the right,'' he said, ''you don't know where that road to the right goes, but,'' he says, ''you take it.'' We know where that other one goes.

In the dicussion of Federal spending, the time has come to put to rest the sob sister attempts to portray our desire to get government spending under control as a hardhearted attack on the poor people of America. In the first place, even with the economies that we've proposed, spending for entitlements—benefits paid directily to individuals—will actually increase by one-third over the next five years. And in 1983 non-defense items will amount to more than 70 per cent of total spending.

As Dave Stockman pointed out the other day, we're still subsidizing 95 million meals a day, providing $70 billion in health care to the elderly and poor, some 47 million people. Some 10 million or more are living in subsidized housing. And we're still providing scholarships for a million and a half students. Only here in this city of Oz would a budget this big and this generous be characterized as a miserly attack on the poor.

Now, where do some of these attacks originate? They're coming from the very people whose past policies, all done in the name of compassion, brought us the current recession. Their policies drove up inflation and interest rates, and their policies stifled incentive, creativity, and halted the movement of the poor up the economic ladder. Some of their criticism is perfectly sincere. But let's also understand that some of their criticism comes from those who have a vested interest in a permanent welfare constituency and in government programs that reinforce the dependency of our people.

Well, I would suggest that no one should have a vested interest in poverty or dependency, that these tragedies must never be looked at as a source of votes for politicians or paychecks for bureaucrats. They are blights on our society that we must work to eliminate, not institutionalize.

Now, there are those who will always require help from the

rest of us on a permanent basis, and we'll provide that help. To those with temporary need, we should have programs that are aimed at making them self-sufficient as soon as possible. How can limited government and fiscal restraint be equated with lack of compassion for the poor? How can a tax break that puts a little more money in the weekly paychecks of working people be seen as an attack on the needy?

Since when do we in America believe that our society is made up of two diametrically opposed classes—one rich, one poor— both in a permanent state of conflict and neither able to get ahead except at the expense of the other? Since when do we in America accept this alien and discredited theory of social and class warfare? Since when do we in America endorse the politics of envy and division?

When we reformed the welfare system in California and got the cheaters and the undeserving off the welfare rolls, instead of hurting the poor we were able to increase their benefits by more than 40 per cent. By reducing the cost of government, we can continue bringing down inflation, the cruelest of all economic exploitations of the poor and the elderly. And by getting the economy moving again, we can creat a vastly expanded job market that will offer the poor a way out of permanent dependency.

One man who held this office, a President vastly underrated by history, Calvin Coolidge, pointed out that a nation that is united in its belief in the work ethic and its desire for commercial success and economic progress is usually a healthy nation, a nation where it is easier to pursue the higher things in life like the development of science, the cultivation of the arts, the exploration of the great truths of religion and higher learning.

In arguing for economy in government, President Coolidge spoke of the burden of excessive government. He said, "I favor a policy of economy, not because I wish to save money, but because I wish to save people. The men and women of this country who toil are the ones who bear the cost of the government. Every dollar that we save means that their life will be so much the more abundant. Economy is idealism in its most practical form." And this is the message we conservatives can bring to the American people about our economic program. Higher productivity, a larger gross national product, a healthy Dow Jones average—they are our goals and are worthy ones.

But our real concerns are not statistical goals or material gain. We want to expand personal freedom, to renew the American dream for every American. We seek to restore opportunity and reward, to value again personal achievement and individual excellence. We seek to rely on the ingenuity and energy of the American people to better their own lives and those of millions of others around the world.

We can be proud of the fact that a conservative administration has pursued these goals by confronting the nation's economic problems head-on. At the same time, we dealt with one other less publicized but equally grave problem: the serious state of disrepair in our national defenses.

The last Democratic administration had increased real defense spending at a rate of 3.3 percent a year. You know how much inflation was, so they were actually losing ground. By 1980 we had fighter planes that couldn't fly, Navy ships that couldn't leave port, a Rapid Deployment Force that was neither rapid nor deployable and not much of a force.

The protection of this nation's security is the most solemn duty of any President, and that's why I've asked for substantial increases in our defense budget—substantial, but not excessive.

In 1962 President Kennedy's defense budget amounted to 44 per cent of the entire budget. Ours is only 29 per cent. In 1962 President Kennedy's request for military spending was 8.6 per cent of the gross national product. Ours is only 6.3 per cent. The Soviet Union outspends us on defense by 50 percent, an amount equal to 15 per cent of their gross national product. During the campaign I was asked any number of times: If I were faced with a choice of balancing the budget or restoring our national defenses, what would I do? Every time I said, "Restore our defenses." And every time I was applauded.

So, let me be very clear. We will press for further cuts in federal spending. We will protect the tax reductions already passed. We will spend on defense what is necessary for our national security. I have no intention of leading the Republican

68

party into next fall's election on a platform of higher taxes and cut-rate defense. If our opponents want to go to the American people next fall and say, "We're the party that tried to cut spending, we're the party that tried to take away your tax cuts, we're the party that wanted a bargain-basement military and held a fire sale on national security," let's give them all the running room they want.

There are other matters on the political agenda for this coming year, matters I know that you've been discussing during the course of this conference. I hope one of them will be our attempt to give government back to the people. One hundred and thirty-two federal grants-in-aid in 1960 have grown to over 500 in 1981. Our federalism proposal would return the bulk of these programs to state and local governments, where they can be made more responsive to the people.

We're deeply committed to this program, because it has its roots in deep conservative principles. We've talked a long time about revitalizing our system of federalism. Now, with a single bold stroke, we can restore the vigor and health of our state and local governments. This proposal lies at the heart of our legislative agenda for the next year, and we'll need your active support in getting it passed.

There are other issues before us. This administration is unalterably opposed to the forced busing of school children, just as we also support constitutional protection for the right of prayer in our schools. And there is the matter of abortion. We must with calmness and resolve help the vast majority of our fellow Americans understand that the more than 1½ million abortions performed in America in 1980 amount to a great moral evil, an assault on the sacredness of human life.

And, finally, there's the problem of crime, a problem whose gravity cannot be underestimated. This administration has moved in its appointments to the federal bench and in its legislative proposals for bail and parole reform to assist in the battle against the lawless. But we must always remember that our legal system does not need reform so much as it needs transformation. And this cannot occur at just the federal level. It can really occur only when a society as a whole acknowledges principles that lie at the heart of modern conservatism. Right and wrong matters, individuals are responsible for their actions. Society has a right to be protected from those who prey on the innocent.

This, then, is the political agenda before us. Perhaps more than any group, your grassroots leadership, your candidate recruitment and training programs, your long years of hard work and dedication have brought us to this point and made this agenda possible.

We live today in a time of climactic struggle for the human spirit, a time that will tell whether the great civilized ideas of individual liberty, representative government, and the rule of law under God will perish or endure.

Whittaker Chambers, who sought idealism in communism and found only disillusionment, wrote very movingly of his moment of awakening. It was at breakfast, and he was looking at the delicate ear of his tiny baby daughter, and he said that, suddenly, looking at that, he knew that couldn't just be an accident of nature. He said, while he didn't realize it at the time, he knows now that in that moment God had touched his forehead with his finger.

And later he wrote, ''For in this century, within the next decades, will be decided for generations whether all mankind is to become Communist, whether the whole world is to become free, or whether in the struggle civilization as we know it is to be completely destroyed or completely changed. It is our fate to live upon that turning point in history.''

We've already come a long way together. Thank you for all that you've done for me, for the common values we cherish. Join me in a new effort, a new crusade.

Nostalgia has its time and place. Coming here tonight has been a sentimental journey for me, as I'm sure it has been for many of you. But nostalgia isn't enough. The challenge is now. It's time we stopped looking backward at how we got here. We must ask ourselves tonight how we can forge and wield a popular majority from one end of this country to the other, a majority united on basic, positive goals with a platform broad enough and deep enough to endure long into the future, far

70

beyond the lifespan of any single issue or personality.

We must reach out and appeal to the patriotic and fundamental ideals of average Americans who do not consider themselves "movement" people, but who respond to the same American ideals that we do. I'm not talking about some vague notion of an abstract, amorphous American mainstream. I'm talking about "Main Street" Americans in their millions. They come in all sizes, shapes and colors—blue-collar workers, blacks, Hispanics, shopkeepers, scholars, service people, housewives, and professional men and women. They are the backbone of America, and we can't move America without moving their hearts and minds as well.

Fellow Americans, our duty is before us tonight. Let us go forward, determined to serve selflessly a vision of man with God, government for people, and humanity at peace. For it is now our task to tend and preserve, through the darkest and coldest nights, that "sacred fire of liberty" that President Washington spoke of two centuries ago, a fire that tonight remains a beacon to all the oppressed of the world, shining forth from this kindly, pleasant, greening land we call America.

God bless you, and thank you.

VII

We Will Not Be
Turned Back

FEBRUARY 18, 1983

President Reagan called this address a "state of the Reagan report"—a progress report on how he had fared in realizing the goals of his Presidency.

He expressed pride that during the recession which was coming to an end his administration hadn't panicked; that he had stayed the course. The President expressed satisfaction with his tax and spending cuts, his defense buildup and his efforts to reduce the size and waste of the federal bureaucracy.

He counseled, however, that much remained to be done, and he singled out a number of social issues—crime, education reform, prayer in the schools and abortion—as ones where he hoped to effect changes. He also touted his "New Federalism" program that would consolidate many federal aid programs into block grants to the states and which would "return vital prerogatives to the states."

LADIES AND GENTLEMEN, MR. CHAIRMAN [Representative Mickey Edwards, ACU Chairman], REVEREND CLERGY, I thank you very much for those very kind words, and I thank you all for certainly a most hearty and warm welcome.

I'm grateful to the American Conservative Union, Young Americans for Freedom, *National Review* and *Human Events* for organizing this third annual memorial service for the Democratic platform of 1980. Someone asked me why I wanted to

72

make it three in a row. Well, you know how the Irish love wakes. [Laughter]

But I'm delighted to be back here with you, at your 10th annual conference. In my last two addresses, I've talked about our common perceptions and goals, and I thought I might report to you here tonight on where we stand in achieving those goals—a sort of state of the Reagan report, if you will.

Now, I'm the first to acknowledge that there's a good deal left unfinished on the conservative agenda. Our cleanup crew will need more than two years to deal with the mess left by others for over half a century. But I'm not disheartened. In fact, my attitude about that unfinished agenda isn't very different from that expressed in an anecdote about one of my favorite Presidents, Calvin Coolidge. [Laughter]

Some of you may know that after Cal Coolidge was introduced to the sport of fishing by his Secret Service detail, it got to be quite a passion with him, if you can use that word about "Silent Cal." Anyway, he was once asked by reporters how many fish were in one of his favorite angling places, the River Brule. And Coolidge said the waters were estimated to carry 45,000 trout. And then he said, "I haven't caught them all yet, but I sure have intimidated them."

Well, it's true we haven't brought about every change important to the conscience of a conservative, but we conservatives can take a great deal of honest pride in what we have achieved. In a few minutes I want to talk about just how far we've come and what we need to do to win further victories. But right now, I think a word or two on strategy is in order. You may remember that in the past, I mentioned that it was not our task as conservatives to just point out the mistakes made over all the decades of liberal government, not just to form an able opposition, but to govern, to lead a nation. And I noted this would make new demands upon our movement, upon all of us.

For the first time in half a century, we've developed a whole new cadre of young conservatives in government. We've shown that conservatives can do more than criticize; we've shown that we can govern and move our legislation through the Congress.

Now, I know there's concern over attempts to roll back some

73

of the gains that we've made. And it seems to me that here we ought to give some thought to strategy—to making sure that we stop and think before we act. For example, some of our critics have been saying recently that they want to take back the people's third-year tax cut and abolish tax indexing. And some others, including members of my staff, wanted immediately to open up a verbal barrage against them. Well, I hope you know that sometimes it's better if a President doesn't say exactly what's on his mind. There's an old story about a farmer and a lawyer that illustrates my point.

It seems that these two got into a pretty bad collison, a traffic accient. They both got out of their cars. The farmer took one look at the lawyer, and walked back to his car, got a package, brought it back. There was a bottle inside, and he said, "Here, you look pretty shook up. I think you ought to take a nip of this, it'll steady your nerves." Well, the lawyer did. And the farmer said, "You still look a bit pale. How about another?" And the lawyer took another swallow. And under the urging of the farmer, he took another and another and another. And then, finally, he said he was feeling pretty good and asked the farmer if he didn't think that he ought to have a little nip, too. And the farmer said, "Not me, I'm waiting for the State trooper."

I wonder if we can't learn something from that farmer. If our liberal friends really want to head into the next election under the banner of taking away from the American people their first real tax cut in nearly 20 years; if, after peering into their heart of hearts, they feel they must tell the American people that over the next six years they want to reduce the income of the average family by $3,000; and if they want to voice these deeply held convictions in an election year—well, fellow conservatives, who are we to stifle the voices of conscience?

Now, in talking about our legislative agenda, I know that some of you have been disturbed by the notion of standby tax increases in the so-called out-years. Well, I wasn't wild about the idea myself. But the economy is getting better, and I believe these improvements are only the beginning. And with some luck, and if the American people respond with the kind of energy and initiative they've always shown in the past, well, maybe it's time we started thinking about some standby tax cuts, too.

But you know, with regard to the economy, I wonder if our political adversaries haven't once again proved that they're our best allies. They spent the last 16 months or so placing all the responsibility for the state of the economy on our shoulders. And with some help from the media, it's been a pretty impressive campaign. They've created quite an image—we're responsibile for the economy.

Well, I assume that we're responsible then for inflation which, after back-to-back years in double digits before we got here, has now been reduced to 3.9 percent in 1982. And for the last three months of the year, it ran at only 1.1 percent. In 1982 real wages increased for the first time in three years. Interest rates, as you've already been told, have dropped dramatically, with the prime rate shrinking by nearly 50 percent. And in December, the index of leading indicators was a full 6.3 percent above last March's low point and has risen in eight of the last nine months. Last month housing starts were up 95 percent and building permits 88 percent over the last year at this time. New home sales are up to by 54 percent since April, and inventories of unsold homes are at the lowest levels in more than a decade. Auto production this quarter is scheduled to increase by 22 percent, and General Motors alone is putting 21,400 of their workers back on the jobs. Last month's sharp decline in the unemployment rate was the most heartening sign of all. It would have taken a $5 billion jobs bill to reduce unemployment by the same amount—and it didn't cost us anything.

It's time to admit our guilt, time we admitted that our liberal critics have been right all the time. And they should go right on telling the American people that the state of economy is precisely the fault of that wicked creature, Kemp–Roth and its havoc-wreaking twin, Reaganomics.

Let's confess, let's admit that we've turned the corner on the economy. And we're especially proud of one thing: when we hit heavy weather, we didn't panic, we didn't go for fast bromides and quick fixes, the huge tax increases or wage and price controls recommended by so many. And our stubborness, if you want to call it that, will quite literally pay off for every American in the years ahead.

So, let me pledge to you tonight: Carefully, we have set out on the road to recovery. We will not be deterred. We will not be turned back. I reject the policies of the past, the policies of tax and tax, spend and spend, elect and elect. The lesson of these failed policies is clear; I've said this before: you can't drink yourself sober or spend yourself rich, and you can't prime the pump without pumping the prime — as somebody did, like to 21½ percent in 1980.

And a word is in order here on the most historic of all the legislative reforms we've achieved in the last two years—that of tax indexing. You can understand the terror that strikes in the heart of those whose principal constituency is big government. Bracket creep is government's hidden incentive to inflate the currency and bring on inflation, and indexing will end that. It will end those huge, hidden subsidies for bigger and bigger government. In the future, if we get indexing planted firmly as a law of the land, the advocates of big government who want money, more money for their social spending, their social engineering schemes, will have to go to the people and say right out loud: We want more money from your weekly paycheck, so we're raising your taxes. Do that instead of sneaking it out by way of inflation, which they have helped bring on.

So, all the professional Washingtonians, from bureaucrats to lobbyists to the special interest groups, are frightened—plain scared—and they're working overtime to take this one back. Well, I think I speak for all conservatives when I say: tax indexing is nonnegotiable. It's a fight we'll take to the people, and we'll win.

But I think you can see how even this debate shows things are changing for the better. It highlights the essential differences between two philosophies now contending for power in American political life. One is the philosophy of the past—a philosophy that has as its constituents an ill-assorted mix of elitists and special-interest groups who see government as the principal vehicle of social change, who believe that the only thing we have

76

to fear is the people, who must be watched and regulated and superintended from Washington.

On the other hand, our philosophy is at the heart of the new political consensus that emerged in America at the beginning of this decade, one that I believe all—well, I believe it will dominate American politics for many decades. The economic disasters brought about by too much government were the catalysts for this consensus. During the '70s, the American people began to see misdirected, overgrown government as the source of many of our social problems—not the solution.

This new consensus has a view of government that's essentially that of our Founding Fathers—that government is the servant, not the master; that it was meant to maintain order, to protect our nation's safety, but otherwise, in the words of that noted political philosopher, schnozzle Jimmy Durante, "Don't put no constrictions on da people. Leave 'em da heck alone."

The overriding goal during the past two years has been to give the government back to the American people, to make it responsive again to their wishes and desires, to do more than bring about a healthy economy or a growing gross national product. We've truly brought about a quiet revolution in American government.

For too many years, bureaucratic self-interest and political maneuvering held sway over efficiency and honesty in government. Federal dollars were treated as the property of bureaucrats, not taxpayers. Those in the Federal Establishment who pointed to the misuse of those dollars were looked upon as malcontents or troublemakers.

Well, this administration has broken with what was a kind of a buddy system. There have been dramatic turnabouts in some of the more scandal-ridden and wasteful federal agencies and programs. Only a few years ago, the General Service Administration was racked by indictments and report after report of inefficiency and waste. Today at GSA, Jerry Carmen has not only put the whistleblowers back in charge, he's promoted them and given them new responsibilities. Just listen to this little set of figures. Today, General Service Administration work-in-progress time is down from 30 days to seven, even while the

77

agency has sustained budget cuts of 20 percent, office space reductions of 20 percent, and the attrition of 7,000 employees.

At the Government Printing Office, under Dan Sawyer, losses of millions of dollars have suddenly been ended as the workforce was cut through attrition and a hiring freeze, and overtime pay was cut by $6 million in one year alone. The Government publication program, which ran a cumulative loss of $20 million over a three-year period, registered a $3.9 million profit, and the GPO as a whole has experienced a profit of $4.1 million last year.

It is said by some that this administration has turned a blind eye to waste and fraud at the Pentagon while overzealously concentrating on the social programs. Well, at the Pentagon, under Cap Weinberger's leadership and our superb service Secretaries, Jack Marsh, John Lehman, and Verne Orr, we have identified more than a billion dollars in savings on waste and fraud, and, over the next seven years, multiyear procurement and other acquisition initiatives will save us almost $30 billion.

Now, these are only three examples of what we're attempting to do to make government more efficient. The list goes on. We have wielded our inspectors general as a strike force accounting for nearly $17 billion in savings in 18 months, With Peter Grace's help, we've called on top management executives and experts from the private sector to suggest modern management techniques for every aspect of government operations. And with an exciting new project called Reform 88, we're going to streamline and reorganize the processes that control the money, information, personnel, and property of the Federal bureaucracy — the maze through which nearly $2 trillion passes each year and which includes 350 different payroll systems and 1,750 personnel offices.

There is more, much more—from cutting down wasteful travel practices to reducing paperwork, from aggressively pursuing the $40 billion in bad debts owed the Federal Government to reducing publication of more than 70 million copies of wasteful or unnecessary government publications.

But, you know, making government responsive again to the people involves more than eliminating waste and fraud and inefficiency. During the decades when government was intruding into areas where it's neither competent nor needed, it was also ignoring its legitimate and constitutional duties such as preserving the domestic peace and providing for the common defense.

I'll talk about that in a moment. I know you've already heard about that today, some of you. But on the matter of domestic order, a few things need to be said. First of all, it is abundantly clear that much of our crime problem was provoked by a social philosophy that saw man as primarily a creature of his material environment. The same liberal philosophy that saw an era of prosperity and virtue ushered in by changing man's environment through massive Federal spending programs also viewed criminals as the unfortunate products of poor socioeconomic conditions or an underprivileged upbringing. Society, not the individual, they said, was at fault for criminal wrongdoing. We are to blame.

Now, we conservatives have been warning about the crime problem for many years, about that permissive social philosophy that did so much to foster it, about a legal system that seemed to specialize in letting hardened criminals go free. And now we have the means and the power to do something. Let's get to work.

Drug pusher after drug pusher, mobster after mobster has escaped justice by taking advantage of our flawed bail and parole system. Criminals who have committed atrocious acts have cynically utilized the technicalities of the exclusionary rule, a miscarriage of justice unique to our legal system. Indeed, one National Institute of Justice study showed that of those arrested for drug felonies in Los Angeles County in 1981, 32 per cent were back out on the streets because of perceived problems with the exclusionary rule.

Now, the exclusionary rule—that isn't a law that was passed by Congress or a state legislature, it's what is called case law, the result of judicial decisions. If a law enforcement officer obtains evidence as the result of a violation of the laws regarding search and seizure, that evidence cannot be introduced in a trial even if it proves the guilt of the accused. Now, this is hardly punishment of the officer for his violation of legal procedures, and it's only effect, in many cases, is to free someone patently guilty of a crime.

I don't know, maybe I've told you this before, but I have to give you a glaring example of what I've taken too much time to explain here. San Bernardino, California, several years ago: two narcotics agents, based on the evidence they had, obtained a legal warrant to search the home of a man and woman suspected of peddling heroin. They searched the home. They didn't find anything. But as they were leaving, just on a hunch, they turned back to the baby in the crib and took down the diapers, and there was the stash of heroin. The evidence was thrown out of court and the couple went free because the baby hadn't given permission for the violation of its constitutional rights.

Well, this administration has proposed vital reforms of our bail and parole systems and criminal forfeiture and sentencing statutes. These reforms were passed by the Senate 95 to one last year. Our anticrime package never got out of committee in the House of Representatives. Do you see a target there? The American people want these reforms, and they want them now. I'm asking tonight that you mobilize all the powerful resources of this political movement to get these measures passed by the Congress.

On another front, all of you know how vitally important it is for us to reverse the decline in American education, to take responsibility for the education of our children out of the hands of parents and teachers. That's why the Congress must stop dithering. We need those tuition tax credits. We need a voucher system for the parents of disadvantaged children. We need education savings accounts, a sort of IRA for college. And finally— and don't think for a moment I've given up—we need to eliminate that unnecessary and politically engendered Department of Education.

There are other steps we're taking to restore government to its rightful duties, to restore the political consensus upon which this nation was founded. Our Founding Fathers prohibited a Federal establishment of religion, but there is no evidence that they intended to set up a wall of separation between the state and religious belief itself.

The evidence of this is all around us. In the Declaration of Independence, alone, there are no fewer than four mentions of a Supreme Being. "In God We Trust" is engraved on our coinage. The Supreme Court opens its proceedings with a religious invocation. And the Congress opens each day with prayer from its chaplains. The schoolchildren of the United States are entitled to the same privileges as Supreme Court Justices and Congressmen. Join me in persuading the Congress to accede to the overwhelming desire of the American people for a constitutional amendment permitting prayer in our schools.

And finally, on our domestic agenda, there is a subject that weighs heavily on all of us—the tragedy of abortion on demand. This is a grave moral evil and one that requires the fullest discussion on the floors of the House and Senate. As we saw in the last century with the issue of slavery, any attempt by the Congress to stifle or compromise away discussion of important moral issues only further inflames emotions on both sides and leads ultimately to even more social disruption and disunity.

So, tonight, I would ask that the Congress discuss the issue of abortion openly and freely on the floors of the House and Senate. Let those who believe the practice of abortion to be a moral evil to join us in taking this case to our fellow Americans. And let us do so rationally, calmly, and with an honest regard for our fellow Americans.

Speaking for myself, I believe that once implications of abortion on demand are fully aired and understood by the American people, they will resolutely seek its abolition. Now, I know there are many who sincerely believe that limiting the right of abortion violates the freedom of choice of the individual. But if the unborn child is a living entity, then there are two individuals, each with the right to life, liberty, and the pursuit of happiness. Unless and until someone can prove the unborn is not alive—and all medical evidence indicates it is — then we must concede the benefit of the doubt to the unborn infant.

But whether it's cutting spending and taxing, shrinking the size of the deficit, ending overregulation, inefficiency, fraud and waste in government, cracking down on career criminals, revitalizing American education, pressing for prayer and abortion legislation, I think you can see that the agenda we've put before America these past two years has been a conservative one. Oh, and there are two other matters that I think you'd be interested in. First, as part of our federalism effort, next week we will be sending to the Congress our proposal for four megablock grants that will return vital prerogatives to the States where they belong. And second, the Office of Management and Budget will press ahead with new regulations prohibiting the use of Federal tax dollars for purposes of political advocacy.

And these important domestic initiatives have been complemented by the conservative ideas we've brought to the pursuit of foreign policy. In the struggle now going on for the world, we have not been afraid to characterize our adversaries for what they are. We have focused world attention on forced labor on the Soviet pipeline and Soviet repression in Poland and all the other nations that make up what is called the "fourth world"—those living under totalitarian rule who long for freedom.

We publicized the evidence of chemical warfare and other atrocities in Cambodia, which we're now supposed to call Kampuchea, and Afghanistan. We pointed out that totalitarian powers hold a radically different view of morality and human dignity than we do. We must develop a forward strategy for freedom, one based on our hope that someday representative government will be enjoyed by all the people and all the nations of the Earth.

We've been striving to give the world the facts about the international arms race. Ever since our nearly total demobilization after World War II, we in the West have been playing catchup. Yes, there's been an international arms race, as some of the declared Democratic candidates for the Presidency tell us. But let them also tell us, there's only been one side doing the racing.

Those of you in the frontline of the conservative movement can be of special assistance in furthering our strategy for freedom, our fight against totalitarianism. First of all, there is no more important foreign policy initiative in this administration, and none that frightens our adversaries more, than our

82

attempts through our international radios to build constituencies for peace in nations dominated by totalitarian, militaristic regimes. We've proposed to the Congress modest but vitally important expenditures for the Voice of America, Radio Free Europe/Radio Liberty, and Radio Marti. These proposals stalled last year, but with your help we can get them through the Congress this year. And believe me, nothing could mean more to the Poles, Lithuanians, Cubans, and all the millions of others living in that fourth world.

Now, it would be also unconscionable during any discussion of the need for candor in our foriegn policy not to mention here the tragic event that last year shocked the world—the attack on His Holiness, Pope John Paul II—an act of unspeakable evil, an assault on man and God. It was an international outrage and merits the fullest possible investigation. Tonight, I want to take this opportunity to applaud the courage and resourcefulness of the Government of Italy in bringing this matter to the attention of the world. And, contrary to what some have suggested, you can depend on it, there is no one on our side that is acting embarrassed or feeling embarrassed because they're going ahead with that investigation. We mean to help them.

And, now, Cap, you can breathe easy, because here we come. We must continue to revitalize and strengthen our Armed Forces. Cap Weinberger's been waging an heroic battle on this front. I'm asking you, the conservative leaders here tonight, to make support for our defense buildup one of your top priorities.

But besides progress in furthering all of these items on the conservative agenda, something else is occuring—something that someday we conservatives many be very proud happened under our leadership. Even with all our recent economic hardships, I believe a feeling of optimism is now entering the American consciousness, a belief that the days of division and discord are behind us and that an era of unity and national revewal is upon us.

A vivid reminder of how our nation has learned and grown and transcended the tragedies of the past was given to us here in Washington only a few months ago. Last November, on the Mall, between the Lincoln Memorial and the Washington

Monument, a new memorial was dedicated—one of dark, low-lying walls inscribed with the names of those who gave their lives in the Vietnam conflict. Soon, there will be added a sculpture of three infantrymen representing different racial and ethnic backgrounds.

During the dedication ceremonies, the rolls of the missing and dead were read for three days, morning till night, in a candlelight ceremony at the National Cathedral. And those veterans of Vietnam who never were welcomed home with speeches and bands, but who were defeated in battle and were heroes as surely as any who ever fought in a noble cause, staged their own parade on Constitution Avenue.

As America watched them, some in wheelchairs, all of them proud, there was a feeling that as a nation we were coming together, coming together again, and that we had at long last brought the boys home.

"A lot of healing...went on," said Jan Scruggs, the wounded combat veteran who helped organize support for the memorial. And then there was this newspaper account that appeared after the ceremonies. I'd like to read it to you.

"Yesterday, crowds returned to the memorial. Among them was Herbie Petit, a machinist and former marine from New Orleans. 'Last night,' he said, standing near the wall, 'I went out to dinner with some ex-marines. There was also a group of college students in the restaurant. We started talking to each other, and before we left, they stood up and cheered. 'The whole week,' Petit said, his eyes red, 'it was worth it just for that.' "

It has been worth it. We Americans have learned again to listen to each other, to trust each other. We've learned that government owes the people an explanation and needs their support for its actions at home and abroad. And we've learned —and I pray this time for good—that we must never again send our young men to fight and die in conflicts that our leaders are not prepared to win.

Yet, the most valuable lesson of all, the preciousness of human freedom, has been relearned not just by Americans but all the people of the world. It is "the stark lesson" that Truong Nhu Tang, one of the founders of the National Liberation Front, a former Viet Cong minister and vice-minister of the postwar Vietnamese Communist government, spoke of recently when he explained why he fled Vietnam for freedom. "No previous regime in my country," he wrote about the concentration camps and boat people of Vietnam, "brought such numbers of people to such desperation. Not the military dictators, not the colonialists, not even the ancient Chinese warlords. It is a lesson that my compatriots and I learned through witnessing and through suffering in our own lives the fate of our countrymen. It is a lesson that must eventually move the conscience of the world." This man who had fought on the other side learned the value of freedom only after helping to destroy it and seeing those who had had to give it up.

The task that has fallen to us as Americans is to move the conscience of the world, to keep alive the hope and dream of freedom. For if we fail or falter, there'll be no place for the world's oppressed to flee to. This is not a role we sought. We preach no manifest destiny. But like the Americans who brought a new nation into the world 200 years ago, history has asked much of us in our time. Much we've already given; much more we must be prepared to give.

This is not a task we shrink from; it's a task we welcome. For with the privilege of living in this kindly, pleasant, greening land called America, this land of generous spirit and great ideals, there is also a destiny and a duty, a call to preserve and hold in sacred trust mankind's age-old aspirations of peace and freedom and a better life for generations to come.

God bless you all, and thank you for what you're doing.

VIII

Our Noble Vision: An Opportunity Society for All

MARCH 2, 1984

This address was made at the high water mark of Ronald Reagan's presidency. With the recession over, the economy on the rebound and the President's popularity also on the rise, Mr. Reagan looked forward with confidence to the 1984 election.

Following a reprise of his Administration's accomplishments, the President enumerated several unrealized goals, and asked for help in enacting them. Among them were the omnibus crime bill, eliminating wasteful federal spending identified by the Grace Commission, a balanced budget amendment, a line item veto, and a reform of the tax system.

His vision, Mr. Reagan said, was of a dynamic, growing economy and an opportunity society in which all Americans — including the unborn threatened by the scourge of abortion — could realize their dreams.

M R. VICE PRESIDENT, MEMBERS OF THE CONGRESS, MEMBERS OF THE CABINET AND DISTINGUISHED LADIES AND GENTLEMEN. I just want to say thank you to Mickey Edwards— I'm honored to stand beside this fine Congressman from Oklahoma and ACU's great leader.

Seeing the size of your gathering here this evening, the exciting program that you've planned, and the media attention you're drawing, and seeing and feeling the drive, energy, and

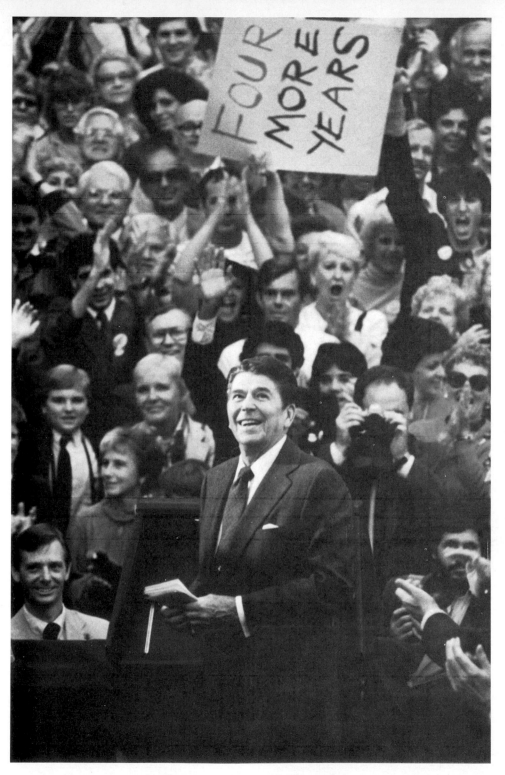

On the campaign trail, 1984

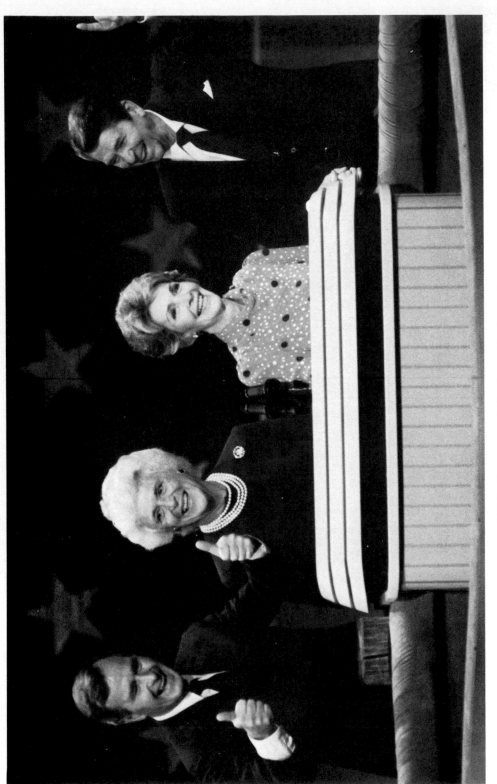

With George and Barbara Bush at the 1984 Republican Convention.

Westward Ho!

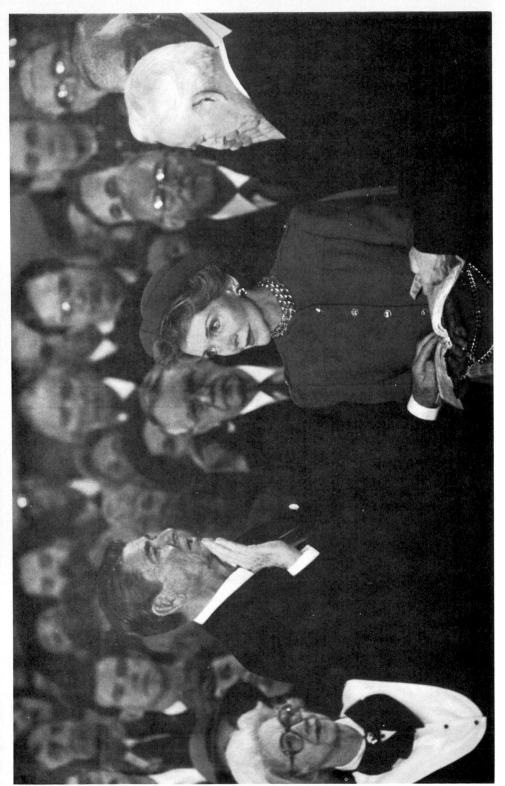

Taking the oath of office, January 1985

Speaking at CPAC 1986. (L. to r.) Tom Winter, editor of *Human Events*, Linda Chavez and Comedian Yakov Smirnov

On the **DMZ** in Korea

President and Mrs. Reagan with ACU chairman
David Keene and Diana Keene

With Margaret Thatcher

intellectual force that's coming to our cause from the American Conservative Union, Young Americans for Freedom, *Human Events*, and *National Review*, I believe the proof is undeniable: The conservative movement is alive and well, and you are giving America a new lease on life.

It is true that many of you are helping now in our Administration. And we're going to add one more in the next few days, because coming to the West Wing, there on our staff, will be the man that organized the first four of these dinners — Frank Donatelli.

We've been together through many struggles. We've known the agony of defeat. And recently, we've seen public support begin to swell behind our banner. What we worked so long and hard to win was good, but hardly good enough. So, in expressing my pride and affection for this good family, for our family, may I say not only Happy Anniversary, ACU, but also, long live the revolution.

The mission of this conference is a mission of principle: It is a mission of commitment, and it must and will be a mission of victory. Color our cause with courage and confidence. We offer an optimistic society. More than 200 years after the patriots fired that first shot heard 'round the world, one revolutionary idea still burns in the hearts of men and women everywhere: A society where man is not beholden to government; government is beholden to man.

The difference between the path toward greater freedom or bigger government is the difference between success and failure; between opportunity and coercion; between faith in a glorious future and fear of mediocrity and despair; between respecting people as adults, each with a spark of greatness, and treating them as helpless children to be forever dependent; between a drab, materialistic world where Big Brother rules by promises to special interest groups, and a world of adventure where everyday people set their sights on impossible dreams, distant stars, and the Kingdom of God. We have the true message of hope for America.

In *Year of Decision, 1846*, Bernard DeVoto explained what drove our ancestors to conquer the West, create a nation, and

87

open up a continent. If you take away the dream, you take away the power of the spirit. If you take away the belief in a greater future, you cannot explain America—that we're a people who believed there was a promised land; we were a people who believed we were chosen by God to create a greater world.

Well, I think we're remembering those bedrock beliefs which motivate our progress. A spirit of renewal is spreading across this land. We even have a pro-conservative newspaper in the Nation's Capital [the Washington *Times*]. And, if I may just interject, I understand that [*Times* Editor and Publisher] Jim Whalen will be honored by your group tomorrow night, and that's wonderful news and well deserved.

I think America is better off than we were three years ago because we've stopped placing our faith in more government programs. We're restoring our faith in the greatest resource this nation has—the mighty spirit of free people under God. It was you who reminded Washington that we are a government of, by, and for the people, not the other way around. It was you who said it is time to put earnings back in the hands of the people, time to put trust back in the hands of the people, time to put America back in the hands of the people.

And this is what we're trying to do. Our critics are not pleased, but I hope we'll be forgiven this small observation: The spendthrifts who mangled America with the nightmare of double-digit inflation, record interest rates, unfair tax increases, too much regulation, credit controls, farm embargoes, gas lines, no-growth at home, weakness abroad, and phony excuses about "malaise" are the last people who should be giving sermonettes about fairness and compassion.

Their failures were not caused by erratic weather patterns, unusual rotations of the moon, or by the personality of my predecessor. They were caused by misguided policies and misunderstanding human nature. Believe me, you cannot create a desert, hand a person a cup of water, and call that compassion. You cannot pour billions of dollars into make-work jobs while destroying the economy that supports them and call that opportunity. And you cannot build up years of dependence on government and dare call that hope.

But apparently nothing bothers our liberal friends. The same expertise that told them their policies must succeed convinced them that our program spelled economic Armageddon. first they blamed the recession on our tax cuts. The trouble is, our tax cuts hadn't started yet. They also warned that when our tax program passed, America would face runaway inflation, record interest rates, and a collapse of confidence. Well, at least they got part of it right. Our program passed, and we witnessed a collapse all right. A collapse of inflation from 12.4 down to about 4 percent; a collapse of the prime interest rate from over 21 percent to 11; and a new surge of confidence in stocks and bonds.

5They warned that decontrolling the price of oil would send the cost of gas at the pumps skyrocketing. We decontrolled, and the price is lower today than it was three years ago when we decontrolled.

And then they said that recovery couldn't come, or would be too feeble to notice. Well, from strong growth in housing to autos, construction, and high technology, from a rebirth of productivity to the fastest drop in unemployment in over 30 years, we have one of the strongest recoveries in decades. And we'll keep it strong if they'll get out of the way.

Pardon me if I add something here. You know, I did get a kick out of watching on TV the door-to-door campaigning in New Hampshire. I got to see some of the homes the people have been able to buy since we brought interest rates down. Incidentally, I'm sure all of you have read or seen on the air that in the month of January our sale of new houses dropped, and dropped to a great percent—about a 9 percent drop below what it was the previous month. Only 688,000 new homes were sold in January. But they didn't add that that drop was only from the sales in December, and beyond that it was the highest number that had been sold since 1979 in a single month.

But our critics moan the recovery can't last. Those awful tax cuts haven't sparked business investment; private borrowers are being crowded out of the capital markets. Well, if that's true, how did the venture capital industry raise four times as much capital in 1983 as it did in 1980? How could real, fixed business investment increase by a 13-percent rate last year, the fastest rate in any recovery in the past 30 years? And how could funds raised in the equity markets zoom from $16.8 billion in 1983—or in 1982, to $36.6 billion in 1983? Still another record.

Now, all this means more growth, more jobs, more opportunities, and a more competitive America. Now, lately, the pessimists have been sounding a new alarm: the dollar is so strong, they say, that exporters can't export, and we'll have no chance for lasting growth.

Well, the facts are—as Secretary [of the Treasury] Don Regan has pointed out—the dollar is strong because of people's confidence in our currency, our low rate of inflation, and the incentives to invest in the United States. No American should undermine confidence in the nation's currency. A strong dollar is one of our greatest weapons against inflation. Anyone who doubts the value of a strong currency should look at the postwar performances of Japan, Switzerland, and West Germany.

Yes, we have a trade deficit, but this isn't entirely new. The United States had a merchandise trade deficit in almost all of the years between 1790 and 1875. I remember them well. 'Course, I was only a boy at the time.

But that was when our economy grew into one of the largest and strongest in the world. Rising incomes have given us the ability to increase purchases from abroad. The U.S. economy is serving as an engine for worldwide recovery, and this will translate into greater demands for our own goods. But even with our current trade deficits, exports of goods and services have made a greater contribution to this recovery than to any previous recovery in the postwar period.

The critics were wrong on inflation, wrong on interest rates, wrong on the recovery, and I believe they'll be wrong on the deficit, too, if the Congress will get spending under control. If optimism were a national disease, they'd be immune for life. Isn't it time that we said no to those who keep saying no to America? If the sourpuss set cannot believe in our nation and her people, then let them stand aside and we will get the job done.

In fairness, I'll admit our critics are worried sick about the future of the economy. They're worried it might keep getting better and better.

Now, those who deal in a world of numbers cannot predict the progress of the human mind, the drive and energy of the spirit, or the power of incentives. We're beginning an industrial renaissance which most experts never saw coming. It started with the 1978 capital gains tax reduction—passed over the objections of the last administration—and which was then made greater by our own tax reductions in 1981.

Incentives laid the seeds for the great growth in venture capital which helped set off the revolution in high technology. Sunrise industries, such as computers, micro-electronics, robotics, and fiber optics—all are creating a new world of opportunities. And as our knowledge expands, business investment is stimulated to modernize older industries with the newer technologies.

Dr. Robert Jastrow, chairman of the first NASA lunar exploration committee, believes the potential in our high-tech industries for new jobs and economic growth is mind-boggling. A year ago, he predicted the computer industry would double in size by 1986, becoming America's biggest business. And now we're seeing the knowledge and benefits of high technology being put to use in medicine, bringing new hope to millions who suffer handicaps and disabilities.

Visionaries see infinite possibilities for new economic growth in America's next frontier—space. Our challenge of building a permanently manned space station, and of further exploration, can open up entire new industries. Products from metal alloys to lifesaving medicines—these can immensely improve our environment and life on Earth.

All our space-related activities must begin with the transportation to get there. This is an area of American technological leadership, and I intend to make sure we keep that edge. That's why I've asked Transportation Secretary Elizabeth Dole to start immediately promoting private sector investment in commercial, unmanned space boosters—the powerful rockets that carry satellites into orbit. With these boosters, and a thriving commercial launch industry, American private enterprise will be

91

blasting off toward new horizons of hope, adventure, and progress—a future that will dazzle our imaginations and lift our spirits.

An opportunity society awaits us. We need only believe in ourselves and give men and women of faith, courage, and vision the freedom to build it. Let others run down America and seek to punish success. Let them call you greedy for not wanting government to take more and more of your earnings. Let them defend their tombstone society of wage and price guidelines, mandatory quotas, tax increases, planned shortages, and shared sacrifices.

We want no part of that mess, thank you very much. We will encourage all Americans—men and women, young and old, individuals of every race, creed, and color—to succeed and be healthy, happy, and whole. This is our goal. We see America not falling behind, but moving ahead; our citizens not fearful and divided, but confident and united by shared values of faith, family, work, neighborhood, peace and freedom.

An opportunity society begins with growth, and that means incentives. As I told the people of Iowa last week, my sympathies are with the taxpayers, not the tax-spenders. I consider stopping them from taking more of your earnings an economic responsibility and a moral obligation. I will not permit an anti-growth coalition to jeopardize this recovery. If they get their way, they'll charge everything on your "Taxpayers Express Card." And believe me, they never leave home without it.

As good conservatives, we were brought up to oppose deficits. But sometimes I think some have forgotten why. We were against deficit spending. Those who would be heroes trying to reduce deficits by raising taxes are not heroes. They have not addressed the point I made in the State of the Union: whether government borrows or increases taxes, it will be taking the same amount of money from the private economy and, either way, that's too much.

We must bring down government spending to a level where it cannot interfere with the ability of the economy to grow. The Congress must stop fiddling and pass a constitutional amendment requiring a balanced federal budget. With strong support

92

from many of you here, we nearly scored a great victory in 1982. It's time to try again. We also seek a line-item veto to prevent pork barrel projects from passing just because they're attached to otherwise good legislation. I'm sure we're united by one goal. The Grace commission identified billions of dollars in wasteful government spending. And I believe the Congress has a responsibility to work with us and eliminate that waste wherever it exists.

Combining these spending restraints with another key reform will make America's economy the undisputed leader for innovation, growth, and opportunity. I'm talking about simplification of the entire tax system. We can make taxes more fair, easier to understand and, more important, we can greatly increase incentives by bringing personal tax rates down. If we can reduce personal tax rates as dramatically as we've reduced capital gains taxes, the underground economy will shrink, the whole world will beat a path to our door, and no one will hold America back. This is the real blueprint for a brighter future and declining deficits.

But economic opportunities can only flourish if the values at the foundation of our society and freedom remain strong and secure. Our families and friends must be able to live and work without always being afraid. Americans are sick and tired of law-abiding people getting mugged, robbed, and raped, while dangerous criminals get off scot-free.

We have a comprehensive crime bill to correct this. It would put an end to the era of coddling criminals, and it's been passed by the Senate. But the legislation is bottled up in the House. Now, maybe it's time they heard from a few of you—a few million of you. You know, you don't have to make them see the light; just make them feel the heat. I hope you realize that in my comments about some of the shortcomings of the Congress, believe me, tonight present company is excepted.

Strengthening values also demands a national commitment to excellence in education. If we are to pioneer a revolution in technology, meet challenges of the space age, and preserve values of courage, responsibility, integrity, and love, then we can't afford a generation of children hooked on cocaine and unable to read or write. Conservatives have pointed out for years that while federal spending on education was soaring, aptitude scores were going steadily down. Look at the case of New Hampshire. It ranks dead last in state spending on education, but its students have the highest SAT scores among those states where at least half the students take the test. And they've maintained that honor for more than 10 years. America's schools don't need new spending programs; they need tougher standards, more homework, merit pay for teachers, discipline, and parents back in charge.

Now there's another important reform to be voted on soon in the Senate. . . . Let us come together, citizens of all faiths, to pray, march, and mobilize every force we have so the God who loves us can be welcomed back into our children's classrooms. I'm gratified that Congressman Newt Gingrich [R.-Ga.] is organizing a rally on the Capitol steps in support of our prayer in school amendment. Please be there if you can, and please send the message loud and clear that God never should have been expelled from America's schools in the first place. And maybe if we can get God and discipline back in our schools, we can get drugs and violence out.

Now, let me make it plain that we seek voluntary school prayer, not a moment of silence. We already have the right to remain silent; we can take the 5th Amendment.

But as we go on, we must redouble our efforts to redress a national tragedy. Since the *Roe* v. *Wade* decision, 15 million unborn children have been lost—15 million children who will never laugh, never sing, never know the joy of human love, will never strive to heal the sick or feed the poor or make peace among nations. They've been denied the most basic of human rights, and we're all the poorer for their loss.

Not long ago I received a letter from a young woman named Kim. She was born with the birth defect, spina bifida, and given little chance to live. But her parents were willing to try a difficult and risky operation on her spine. It worked. And Kim wrote me: ''I am now 24 years old. I do have some medical problems due to my birth defect. I have a lot of problems with my legs. But I'm walking. I can talk. I went to grade and high school, plus

94

one year of college. I thank God every day for my parents and my life." And Kim said, "I wouldn't change it if I could."

Life was her greatest opportunity, and she's made the most of it. An opportunity society for all, reaching for its future with confidence, sustained by faith, fair play, and a conviction that good and courageous people flourish when they're free—this is the noble vision we share, a vision of a strong and prosperous America, at peace with itself and the world. Just as America has always been synonymous with freedom, so, too, should we become the symbol of peace across the Earth. I'm confident we can keep faith with that mission.

Peace with freedom is our highest aspiration—a lasting peace anchored by courage, realism, and unity. We've stressed our willingness to meet the Soviets halfway in talks on strategic weapons. But as Commander in Chief, I have an obligation to protect this country, and I will never allow political expediency to influence these crucial negotiations.

We should remember that our defense capability was allowed to deteriorate for many years. Only when our arms are certain beyond doubt can we be certain beyond doubt that they will never be used. President John F. Kennedy spoke those words in 1961. Too many who admired him have forgotten that the price of peace is dear. But some members of his party have not, and I am proud to have one of them, a brilliant patriot, Jeane Kirkpatrick, by my side.

And I deeply appreciate your patriotic support for rebuilding our defenses. We're just beginning to restore our capability to meet present and future security needs. I am open to suggestions for budget savings, but defense is not just another federal program. It is solely the responsibility of the federal government. It is its prime responsibility. So, our first responsibility is to keep America strong enough to remain free, secure, and at peace, and I intend to make sure that we do just that.

America's foreign policy supports freedom, democracy, and human dignity for all mankind, and we make no apologies for it. The opportunity society that we want for ourselves we also want for others, not because we're imposing our system on others but because those opportunities belong to all people as God-given

95

birthrights and because by promoting democracy and economic opportunity we make peace more secure.

Democratic nations do not wage war on their neighbors. But make no mistake, those who would hang a "Do Not Disturb" sign on our shores, those who would weaken America or give Castro's terrorists free rein to bring violence closer and closer to our borders are doing no service to the cause of peace.

Fellow citizens, fellow conservatives, our time has come again. This is our moment. Let us unite, shoulder to shoulder, behind one mighty banner for freedom. And let us go forward from here not with some faint hope that our cause is not yet lost; let us go forward confident that the American people share our values, and that together we will be victorious.

And in those moments when we grow tired, when our struggle seems hard, remember what Eric Liddell, Scotland's Olympic champion runner, said in *Chariots of Fire*: "So where does the power come from to see the race to its end? From within. God made me for a purpose, and I will run for His pleasure."

If we trust in Him, keep His word, and live our lives for His pleasure, He'll give us the power we need—power to fight the good fight, to finish the race and to keep the faith.

Thank you very much. God bless you and God bless America.

IX

Creators of The Future
MARCH 8, 1985

In this address, delivered less than two months after his
second inauguration, President Reagan spoke of achieving a second American revolution that would truly accomplish the aim of the first—to make government beholden to
the people.

He extended his gaze past domestic concerns, however,
to contemplate the larger struggle of freedom against
tyranny in the world, and proclaimed that the forces of
freedom were on the offensive. The repeal of the Brezhnev
Doctrine, he said, had begun in the liberation of Grenada
and would continue in victories by the democratic resistance in Angola and Nicaragua. The President also gave a
strong defense of his Strategic Defense Initiative as a
means of ensuring a future without nuclear war.

The forces of freedom had caught Shakespeare's flood
tide which "leads on to fortune," and it was the conservatives who were now the "creators of the future."

THANK YOU ALL VERY MUCH. Thank you, Vice Chairman [of
the American Conservative Union James A.] Linen, for
those very kind words. I'm grateful to the American Conservative Union, Young Americans for Freedom, *National Review,
Human Events*, for organizing this wonderful evening. When you
work in the White House, you don't get to see your old friends
as much as you'd like. And I always see the Conservative Political Action Conference speech as my opportunity to "dance
with the one that brung ya."

There's so much I want to talk about tonight. I've been thinking, in the weeks since the inauguration, that we are at an especially dramatic turning point in American history. And just putting it all together in my mind, I've been reviewing the elements that have led to this moment.

Ever since F.D.R. and the New Deal, the opposition party, and particularly those of a liberal persuasion, have dominated the political debate. Their ideas were new; they had momentum; they captured the imagination of the American people. The left held sway for a long time. There was a right, but it was, by the '40s and '50s, diffuse and scattered, without a unifying voice.

But in 1964 came a voice in the wilderness—Barry Goldwater; the great Barry Goldwater, the first major party candidate of our time who was a true-blue, undiluted conservative. He spoke from principle, and he offered vision. Freedom—he spoke of freedom: freedom from the government's increasing demands on the family purse, freedom from the government's increasing usurpation of individual rights and responsibilities, freedom from the leaders who told us the price of world peace is continued acquiescence to totalitarianism. He was ahead of his time. When he ran for President, he won six states and lost 44. But his candidacy worked as a precursor of things to come.

A new movement was stirring. And in the 1960's Young Americans for Freedom is born; *National Review* gains readership and prestige in the intellectual community; *Human Events* becomes a major voice on the cutting edge. In the '70s the anti-tax movement begins. Actually, it was much more than an anti-tax movement, just as the Boston Tea Party was much more than an anti-tax initiative. In the late '70s Proposition 13 and the Sagebrush Rebellion; in 1980, for the first time in 28 years, a Republican Senate is elected; so, may I say, is a conservative President. In 1984 that conservative administration is re-elected in a 49-state sweep. And the day the votes came in, I thought of Walt Whitman: "I hear America singing."

This great turn from left to right was not just a case of the pendulum swinging—first, the left hold sway and then the right, and here comes the left again. The truth is, conservative thought is no longer over here on the right; it's the mainstream now.

And the tide of history is moving irresistibly in our direction. Why? Because the other side is virtually bankrupt of ideas. It has nothing more to say, nothing to add to the debate. It has spent its intellectual capital, such as it was, and it has done its deeds.

Now, we're not in power because they failed to gain electoral support over the past 50 years. They did win support. And the result was chaos, weakness, and drift. Ultimately, though, their failures yielded one great thing—us guys. We in this room are not simply profiting from their bankruptcy; we are where we are because we're winning the contest of ideas. In fact, in the past decade, all of a sudden, quietly, mysteriously, the Republican party has become the party of ideas.

We became the party of the most brilliant and dynamic young minds. I remember them, just a few years ago, running around scrawling Laffer curves on table napkins, going to symposia and talking about how social programs did not eradicate poverty, but entrenched it; writing studies on why the latest weird and unnatural idea from the social engineers is weird and unnatural. You were there. They were your ideas, your symposia, your books, and usually somebody else's table napkins.

All of a sudden, Republicans were not defenders of the status quo but creators of the future. They were looking at tomorrow with all the single-mindedness of an inventor. In fact, they reminded me of the American inventors of the 19th and 20th centuries who filled the world with light and recorded sound.

The new conservatives made anew the connection between economic justice and economic growth. Growth in the economy would not only create jobs and paychecks, they said; it would enhance familial stability and encourage a healthy optimism about the future. Lower those tax rates, they said, and let the economy become the engine of our dreams. Pull back regulations, and encourage free and open competition. Let the men and women of the marketplace decide what they want.

But along with that, perhaps the greatest triumph of modern conservatism has been to stop allowing the left to put the average American on the moral defensive. By average American I mean the good, decent, rambunctious, and creative people who raise the families, go to church, and help out when the local library holds a fundraiser; people who have a stake in the community because they are the community.

These people had held true to certain beliefs and principles that for 20 years the intelligentsia were telling us were hopelessly out of date, utterly trite, and reactionary. You want prayer in the schools? How primitive, they said. You oppose abortion? How oppressive, how antimodern. The normal was portrayed as eccentric, and only the abnormal was worthy of emulation. The irreverent was celebrated, but only irreverence about certain things: irreverence toward, say, organized religion, yes; irreverence toward established liberalism, not too much of that. They celebrated their courage in taking on safe targets and patted each other on the back for slinging stones at a confused Goliath, who was too demoralized and really too good to fight back.

But now one simply senses it. The American people are no longer on the defensive. I believe the conservative movement deserves some credit for this. You spoke for the permanent against the merely prevalent, and ultimately you prevailed.

I believe we conservatives have captured the moment, captured the imagination of the American people. And what now? What are we to do with our success? Well, right now, with conservative thought accepted as mainstream thought and with the people of our country leading the fight to freedom, now we must move.

You remember your Shakespeare: "There is a tide in the affairs of men which, taken at the flood, leads on to fortune. Omitted, all the voyage of their life is bound in shallows and in miseries. On such a full sea are we now afloat. And we must take the current when it serves, or lose our ventures." I spoke in the —[applause]. It's typical, isn't it? I just quoted a great writer, but as an actor, I get the bow. [Laughter]

I spoke in the State of the Union of a second American revolution, and now is the time to launch that revolution and see that it takes hold. If we move decisively, these years will not be just a

100

passing era of good feeling, not just a few good years, but a true golden age of freedom.

The moment is ours, and we must seize it. There's work to do. We must prolong and protect our growing prosperity so that it doesn't become just a passing phase, a natural adjustment between periods of recession. We must move further to provide incentives and make America the investment capital of the world.

We must institute a fair tax system and turn the current one on its ear. I believe there is natural support in our country for a simplified tax system, with still lower tax rates but a broader base, with everyone paying their fair share and no more. We must eliminate unproductive tax shelters. Again, there is natural support among Americans, because Americans are a fair-minded people.

We must institute enterprise zones and a lower youth minimum wage so we can revitalize distressed areas and teenagers can get jobs. We're going to take our revolution to the people, all of the people. We're going to go to black Americans and members of all minority groups, and we're going to make our case.

Part of being a revolutionary is knowing that you don't have to acquiesce to the tired, old ideas of the past. One such idea is that the opposition party has black America and minority America locked up, that they own black America. Well, let me tell you, they own nothing but the past. The old alignments are no longer legitimate, if they ever were.

We're going to reach out, and we need your help. Conservatives were brought up to hate deficits, and justifiably so. We've long thought there are two things in Washington that are unbalanced—the budget and the liberals.

But we cannot reduce the deficit by raising taxes. And just so that every "i" is dotted and every "t" is crossed, let me repeat tonight for the benefit of those who never seem to get the message: we will not reduce the deficit by raising taxes. We need more taxes like John McLaughlin [Washington executive editor of *National Review*] needs assertiveness training.

Now, whether government borrows or increases taxes, it will

101

be taking the same amount of money from the private economy, and either way, that's too much. We must bring down government spending. We need a constitutional amendment requiring a balanced budget. It's something that 49 states already require —no reason the federal government should be any different.

We need the line-item veto, which 43 governors have—no reason that the President shouldn't. And we have to cut waste. The Grace commission has identified bilions of dollars that are wasted and that we can save.

But the domestic side isn't the only area where we need your help. All of us in this room grew up, or came to adulthood, in a time when the doctrine of Marx and Lenin was coming to divide the world. Ultimately, it came to dominate remorselessly whole parts of it. The Soviet attempt to give legitimacy to its tyranny is expressed in the infamous Brezhnev doctrine, which contends that once a country has fallen into Communist darkness, it can never again be allowed to see the light of freedom.

Well, it occurs to me that history has already begun to repeal that doctrine. It started one day in Grenada. We only did our duty, as a responsible neighbor and a lover of peace, the day we went in and returned the government to the people and rescued our own students. We restored that island to liberty. Yes, it's only a small island, but that's what the world is made of—small islands yearning for freedom.

There's much more to do. Throughout the world the Soviet Union and its agents, client states, and satellites are on the defensive—on the moral defensive, the intellectual defensive, and the political and economic defensive. Freedom movements arise and assert themselves. They're doing so on almost every continent populated by man—in the hills of Afghanistan, in Angola, in Kampuchea, in Central America. In making mention of freedom fighters, all of us are privileged to have in our midst tonight one of the brave commanders who lead the Afghan freedom fighters—Abdul Haq. Abdul Haq, we are with you.

They are our brothers, these freedom fighters, and we owe them our help. I've spoken recently of the freedom fighters of Nicaragua. You know the truth about them. You know who

102

they're fighting and why. They are the moral equal of our Founding Fathers and the brave men and women of the French Resistance. We cannot turn away from them, for the struggle here is not right versus left; it is right versus wrong.

Now, I am against sending troops to Central America. They are simply not needed. Given a chance and the resources, the people of the area can fight their own fight. They have the men and women. They're capable of doing it. They have the people of their country behind them. All they need is our support. All they need is proof that we care as much about the fight for freedom 700 miles from our shores as the Soviets care about the fight against freedom 5,000 miles from theirs. And they need to know that the U.S. supports them with more than just pretty words and good wishes. We need your help on this, and I mean each of you—involved, active, strong, and vocal. And we need more.

All of you know that we're researching nonnuclear technologies that may enable us to prevent nuclear ballistic missiles from reaching U.S. soil or that of our allies. I happen to believe —logic forces me to believe—that this new defense system, the Strategic Defense Initiative, is the most hopeful possibility of our time. Its primary virtue is clear. If anyone ever attacked us, Strategic Defense would be there to protect us. It could conceivably save millions of lives.

SDI has been criticized on the grounds that it might upset any chance of an arms control agreement with the Soviets. But SDI *is* arms control. If SDI is, say 80 percent effective, then it will make any Soviet attack folly. Even partial success in SDI would strengthen deterrence and keep the peace. And if our SDI research is successful, the prospects for real reduction in U.S. and Soviet offensive nuclear forces will be greatly enhanced.

It is said that SDI would deal a blow to the so-called East–West balance of power. Well, let's think about that. The Soviets already are investing roughly as much on strategic defenses as they are on their offensive nuclear forces. This could quickly tip the East–West balance if we had no defense of our own. Would a situation of comparable defenses threaten us? No, for we're not planning on being the first to use force.

As we strive for our goal of eventual elimination of nuclear

103

weapons, each side would retain a certain amount of defensive—or of, I should say, destructive power—a certain number of missiles. But it would not be in our interest, or theirs, to build more and more of them.

Now, one would think our critics on the left would quickly embrace, or at least be open-minded about a system that promises to reduce the size of nuclear missile forces on both sides and to greatly enhance the prospects for real arms reductions. And yet we hear SDI belittled by some with nicknames, or demagogued with charges that it will bring war to the heavens.

They complain that it won't work, which is odd from people who profess to believe in the perfectability of man—machines after all. And man-machines are so much easier to manipulate. They say it won't be 100 percent effective, which is odd, since they don't ask for 100 percent effectiveness in their social experiments. They say SDI is only in the research stage and won't be realized in time to change things. To which, as I said last month, the only reply is: then let's get started.

Now, my point here is not to question the motives of others. But it's difficult to understand how critics can object to exploring the possibility of moving away from exclusive reliance upon nuclear weapons. The truth is, I believe that they find it difficult to embrace any idea that breaks with the past, that breaks with consensus thinking and the common establishment wisdom. In short, they find it difficult and frightening to alter the status quo.

And what are we to do when these so-called opinion leaders of an outworn philosophy are out there on television and in the newspapers with their steady drumbeat of doubt and distaste? Well, when all you have to do to win is rely on the good judgment of the American people, then you're in good shape, because the American people have good judgment. I know it isn't becoming of me, but I like to think that maybe 49 of our 50 states displayed that judgment just a few months ago.

What we have to do, all of us in this room, is get out there and talk about SDI. Explain it, debate it, tell the American people the facts. It may well be the most important work we do in the next few years. And if we try, we'll succeed. So, we have great work ahead of us, big work. But if we do it together and with complete commitment, we can change our country and history forever.

Once during the campaign, I said, "This is a wonderful time to be alive," and I meant that. I meant that we're lucky not to live in pale and timid times. We've been blessed with the opportunity to stand for something—for liberty and freedom and fairness. And these are things worth fighting for, worth devoting our lives to. And we have good reason to be hopeful and optimistic.

We've made much progress already. So, let us go forth with good cheer and stout hearts—happy warriors out to seize back a country and a world to freedom.

Thank you, and God bless you. Thank you very much.

X

Forward For Freedom
JANUARY 30, 1986

Looking ahead in this address to the fall mid-term election, President Reagan warned against "a great danger that lies ahead" — the danger of complacency.

Many conservative programs had been threatened by the Congress, he said, particularly by the House of Representatives, which remained in liberal control. It was essential, he said, that conservatives stop talking in defensive terms of protecting their gains and focus instead on extending those gains to the House.

Conservatives had suffered many setbacks, he said, but it was important that, like the families of the astronauts killed in the recent shuttle tragedy, they redouble their commitment to the cause.

T HANK YOU ALL VERY MUCH, AND MAY I SAY THAT every bit of show business instinct that is within me says that perhaps it would be better if the entertainment followed the speaker. You are a tough act to follow. [The President was referring to the comic routine of Yakov Smirnoff.]

But let me begin by saying how appropriate it is that we honor tonight the Shuttle Seven; all of them were heroes. Each of us is in their debt. And we know now that God holds them close, and we pray He'll comfort their grieving loved ones. And we're aware, too, of our own duty to them and to their memory. We must continue. Other brave Americans must go now where they so valiantly tried to lead—a fitting place, I've always thought, for Americans—"the stars and beyond."

And in some closed societies, a tragedy of this sort would be permanently disheartening, a fatal setback to any such program, followed not by mourning and national recommitment, but by attempts to evade responsibility. Well, not so in a democracy, and not so in America. John Glenn said the other day that after the pad fire that killed three astronauts in 1967, support for the space program skyrocketed among the American people. And that's because here the government does not rule the people; it *is* the people. And ultimately what happens to programs of this sort, and what follows tragedies of this kind, are decisions that belong not to government, but to the people.

The tragedy of the Shuttle Seven will only serve to strengthen the resolve of America to pursue their dream of "the stars and beyond." And anyone who doubts this does not know the history of our land, the wonder of America and her free people, or the meaning of the words "the right stuff."

You know, I called the families yesterday of those seven heroes. Every one of them concluded the remarks between us by saying, "The program must continue; they would have wanted it that way." And it will.

Well, I'm delighted to be here tonight. And I want to extend my heartfelt thanks to the American Conservative Union, along with *Human Events, National Review*, and Young Americans for Freedom for putting on this conference and for extending the invitation.

Tonight my thoughts cannot help but drift back to another conservative audience of more than 20 years ago and a Presidential campaign that the pundits and opinion-makers said then was the death knell for our movement. But just as the opinion leaders had been stunned by Barry Goldwater's nomination, so too they would be shocked by the resiliency of his cause and the political drama to unfold around it: the rise of the New Right and the religious revival of the mid-'70s and the final, triumphant march to Washington in 1980 by conservatives.

And you know, that last event really did come as a shock of

seismic proportions to this city. I can remember reading about a poll that was taken at a Washington National Press Club luncheon in January of 1980 on the eve of the primary season. Those in attendance were asked who would be the next President of the United States. Well, Jimmy Carter got a large number of votes, and so did Teddy Kennedy. But there was one candidate on the Republican side who got so few votes from the wise men of Washington that it wasn't even reported in the lineup. I think it had to do with his conservative leanings. Well, I hope they know I'm not about to change.

But while official Washington always underestimated our cause, some of the shrewder journalists did over the years sense something astir in America. Theodore White said openly, just after Barry Goldwater's campaign: "Some see this as a last adventure in the politics of nostalgia. Others see this Arizonan as a symbol, cast up by the first crest of an early tide, thrown back this once, but bound to come again in greater strength."

And you know, to be here tonight and to be a part of this historic conference, your biggest attention-getter, to look at your program for the next two days and all the important people and discussions, to stand here now with the Presidential seal on this podium, to feel the energy, the almost festive air of this audience, I think you've provided an answer to Teddy White's implicit question about the fate of our movement, the state of our cause. Fellow conservatives, it took us more than 20 years, but who can deny it? We're rockin' and rollin'.

Now, I know a few liberal observers will try to downplay all this. But don't you think they're going to sound a little bit like Yogi Berra on that famous occasion when he said of a restaurant, "It's so crowded, nobody goes there anymore"? And as for those liberals who finally are catching on to the idea that there is a conservative movement, they kind of remind me of a cowboy who was out hiking in the desert one day and came across the Grand Canyon. And he said, "Wow, something sure happened here!"

Well, something has happened in America. In five short years, we have seen the kind of political change rarely seen in a generation on nearly every issue: Federal spending, tax cuts,

108

deregulation, the fight against career criminals and for tough judges, military readiness, resistance to Soviet expansionism, and the need for candor about the struggle between freedom and totalitarianism. The old taboos and superstitions of liberalism have collapsed and all but blown away, to be replaced by a robust and enlightened conservatism, a conservatism that brings with it economic prosperity, personal opportunity, and a shining hope that someday all the peoples of the world—from Afghanistan to Nicaragua to Poland and, yes, to Angola—will know the blessings of liberty and live in the light of freedom.

Those in this room know how often we were told the odds of accomplishing even a small part of this were all against us. I remember my own first visit up to the Hill after the 1980 election, when issues like the tax cuts came up. I met a Congressman there. He was a kind of a big fellow, as I recall—had lots of white hair. He was from the Boston area, I think. Maybe you know him. He smiled very indulgently and told me not to expect too much because I was, to use his words, "in the big leagues now."

But you know, as a conservative, I had an advantage. Back in the hard years, the lean years, when we were forming our political PACs, sending out our fundraising letters, and working for candidate after candidate in campaign after campaign, all of us learned something vital, something important about our country. Something became an article of faith, a faith that sustained us through all the setbacks and the heartache.

You see, we knew then what we know now: that the real big leaguers aren't here in Washington at all; they're out there in the heartland, out in the real America, where folks go to work every day and church every week, where they raise their families and help their neighbors, where they build America and increase her bounty and pass on to each succeeding generation her goodness and splendor. And we knew something else, too: that the folks out there in real America pretty much see things our way and that all we ever have to do to get them involved is to be brave enough to trust them with the truth and bold enough to ask for their help.

And it's here we find the explanation for the success of the last

109

five years, the reason why on issue after issue the liberals in this town have lost and are still losing: they've forgotten who's in charge, who the big leaguers really are.

It reminds me of a favorite little story of mine about a career naval officer who finally got his four stripes, became a captain, and then was given command of a giant battleship. And one night he was out steaming around the Atlantic when he was called from his quarters to the bridge and told about a signal light in the distance. And the captain told the signalman, "Signal them to bear to starboard." And back came the signal from ahead asking—or saying, "*You* bear to starboard." Well, as I say, the captain was very aware that he was commander of a battleship, the biggest thing afloat, the pride of the fleet; and he said "Signal that light again to bear to starboard *now*." "Bear to starboard yourself." Well, the captain decided to give his unknown counterpart a lesson in seagoing humility, so he said, "Signal them again and tell them to bear to starboard. I am a battleship." And back came the signal, "Bear to starboard yourself. I'm a lighthouse."

Well, the American people have turned out to be just what the forefathers thought they would be when they made them the final arbiter of political power: a lighthouse to the ship of state, a source of good judgment and common sense signaling a course to starboard. But you who are not nautical-minded know that starboard is to the right, don't you?

But I come here tonight not just to celebrate these successes of our past, but also to strike a serious, even somber, note to remind each of you not only of how far we have come together but how tragic it would be if we suddenly cast aside in a moment of dreadful folly all our hopes for a safe America and a freer world. My fellow conservatives, I want to speak to you tonight about our movement and a great danger that lies ahead.

Now, some of you may think I'm reacting here to claims that 1985 was a disappointing or, at best, a mediocre year for conservatives. In fact, I want to take sharp issue with this, suggest to you that those claims themselves are evidence of the broader problem I'm talking about: the danger of growing soft with victory, of losing perspective when things go our way too often, of failing to appreciate success when it occurs or seeing danger when it looms.

First, let's talk about 1985 and three legislative victories whose strategic significance were both enormous and largely overlooked. Now, some of you who go back with me to that campaign in 1964 can remember how easily the liberals dismissed our warnings then about the dangers of deficit spending. We were told it would bring prosperity. Others of you know how passionately the liberals believed in the use of high and punitive tax rates to redistribute income. And finally, all of us can remember how liberals found in the post-Vietnam syndrome a form of religious exercise, a kind of spiritual ecstasy, however much that syndrome paralyzed American foreign policy and jeopardized freedom.

Now, let me ask you: if someone had come up to you even as late as a few years ago and told you that by 1985 all of these cherished doctrines—a belief in deficit spending, the politics of envy via high tax rates, and the refusal to help those resisting Communist dictatorship—would be formally and publicly rejected in a single 12-month period by the liberal Democrats themselves, wouldn't you have thought that person prone to acute shortages of oxygen in the cerebral hemispheres? That's a kind of bureaucratese for meaning playing without a full deck.

But consider 1985. We saw a de facto balanced budget amendment passed by both Houses of the Congress. We saw a House of Representatives under liberal leadership agree to cut the top marginal tax rate to the 35- to 38-percent range. And we even saw that same House not only approve funds for an insurgency against a Communist government but spontaneously repeal that symbol of liberal isolationism, the Clark amendment.

So, friends and neighbors, salute Halley's Comet. Salute that space shot "U-*ra*-nus" — I'm too old-fashioned to call it "*Ur*-a-nus." I just remember politics in 1985 was also a celestial phenomenon, Steven Spielberg all the way.

Actually, the remarkable year of 1985 at home was a reflection of a broader, even brighter strategic picture. In Europe and Asia, statism and socialism are dying and the free market is

111

growing; and all across the world, the march of democracy continues. Yet, even as I think the tide of history is all but irreversibly turned our way and this strategic picture will continue to improve, we must guard at all costs against an unnecessary but costly tactical defeat ahead. I'm talking, of course, about the election in November.

Now, this isn't going to happen as long as we conservatives will shoulder the burden of our recent successes, if we'll realize how much is at stake this November, forget for the moment the flowers and the sunshine, and summon once again those deep reserves of will and stamina that won for us our first victories. And bear in mind, this will require a supreme effort; our job is going to be even tougher this year. The very years of prosperity and peace that conservative programs have given America may in a strange way actually help those who fought the hardest against them. Good times, after all, tend to favor incumbents and fortify the status quo.

Yet you and I know how unacceptable that status quo is, how much—on everything from right to life, prayer in the schools, enterprise zones, aid to the anti-Communist insurgents — still waits to be done. So, we must go to the record, get the facts to the American people.

The Speaker of the House has already indicated a tax increase is the solution to our problems, and recently another important member of the House leadership echoed his sentiments. Not much has changed on the federal spending either. Sure the liberals are angry about Gramm–Rudman, but they aren't looking realistically at our bloated expenditures, only talking nonsense about shutting down the FBI and the IRS—though I do admit that in mentioning that last point they may be tempting me beyond my strength. And as for defense, let me assure you the liberals haven't changed a bit; they're still looking at America's defense budget with lust in their hearts. A lust to strip it bare and use the funds for more of their social experiments.

Yet, this year we have to work even harder at summoning the vigor to tell the American people the truth and the vigor to ask their help, to remind them that what they do this November will

112

decide whether the days of high taxes and higher spending, the days of economic stagnation and skyrocketing inflation, the days of national malaise and international humiliation, the days of "blame America first" and "inordinate fear of communism" will all come roaring back at us once again. More than that, we must tell the American people that the progress that we've made thus far is not enough, that it'll never be enough until the conservative agenda is enacted—and that means enterprise zones, prayer in the public schools, and protection of the unborn.

And that's why, my fellow conservatives, we have to stop limiting ourselves to talking about holding on to our strength in the Senate and start talking about conservative control of the House of Representatives. That House has been in the hands of our opponents for virtually half a century. Never forget that for those nearly 50 years the liberals had it all their own way in this city and that the loss of such great power is rarely accompanied with graceful acquiescence.

Well, since the liberals are feeling pretty sorry for themselves, and that's why they're anxious about this election. They know that unless they deliver a telling blow this year to conservatism, the 1988 Conservative Political Action Conference will see major Presidential candidates from both parties demanding a chance to appear here and claim the mantle of conservatism.

So, this is our break point; our opponents are pulling out all the stops. And you know, I think it's going to be worthwhile reminding the American people of how desperate the liberals are, how so much of their strength in the House of Representatives, as many as 18 to 23 seats, is due to gerrymandering on a scale unprecedented in modern history. And this is not to mention the outrageous episode in which a legitimately elected Member of the Congress and the people of Indiana's 8th District were disenfranchised in the House of Representatives.

But there's another issue that I also believe vividly illustrates how seriously out of touch the liberals are with the American people. We sometimes forget that no one is more realistic about the nature of the threat to our freedom than the American people themselves. In fact, their intuitive realism is why that "Bear in the Woods" ad some of you can remember from the

113

1984 campaign was so successful. Yes, the American people want an administration that pursues every path to peace, but they also want an administration that is realistic about Soviet expansionism, committed to resisting it, and determined to advance the cause of freedom around the world.

Now, we know what happens when an administration that has illusions about the Soviets takes over. First, there are the illusions, then the surprise and anger when the Soviets do something like invading Afghanistan. Any way you look at it, it heightened tension and the prospects for conflict.

In fact, the liberal conduct of foreign policy reminds me of a little football game that was played at Notre Dame back in 1946, when Notre Dame player Bob Livingstone missed a tackle. And his teammate, all-American Johnny Lujack, screamed, "Livingstone, you so-and-so you," and he went on and on. And then, Coach Frank Leahy said, "Another sacrilege like that, Jonathan Lujack, and you'll be disassociated from our fine Catholic university." Well, in the very next play, Livingstone missed another tackle, and Coach Leahy turned to the bench and said, "Lads, Jonathan Lujack was right about Robert Livingstone." And that's why it's important to go to the record.

I remember a little booklet that came out a few years back. Although it was by the Republican Study Committee and entitled "What's the Matter with Democratic Foreign Policy," it was really about a shrinking group of foreign policy liberals here in Washington. And I just think that if we were able to get some of those choice quotations on issues like Vietnam, Grenada, and Central America before the American people and they were able to see what the Washington liberals really believe about foreign policy, the naivete and confusion of mind, I believe we would shock the American people into repudiating these views once and for all.

And let me interject here two points that I think can be important this year. First, the question of defense spending. During the last few weeks, there've been a number of columns, editorials, or speeches calling for a slash in the military budget and quoting President Eisenhower as justification. President Eisenhower did warn about large concentrations of power like the

114

military–industrial complex, but what's being left out is the context of that quote. In his farewell address to the American people, yes, he did warn us about the danger of an all-powerful military–industrial complex, but he also reminded us America must always be vigilant because "We face a hostile ideology—global in scope, atheistic in character, ruthless in purpose, and insidious in method." The pundits haven't been quoting that part of his speech.

I know there's been a great deal of talk in the media recently about the situation in Southwest Africa and especially Angola. And I know also you'll be having a special guest here tomorrow evening, as I did this morning in the Oval Office. Well, let me just say now it would be inappropriate for me as President to get too specific tonight. But I do want to make a comment here on some recent history and let you draw your own conclusions.

Last September, at the Lomba River in southern Angola, when a force of UNITA rebels met an overwhelmingly superior force of government troops directly supported by the Soviet bloc, the UNITA forces defeated the government troops and drove them and their Communist allies from the field.

In the history of revolutionary struggles or movements for true national liberation, there is often a victory like this that electrifies the world and brings great sympathy and assistance from other nations to those struggling for freedom. Past American Presidents, past American Congresses, and always, of course, the American people have offered help to others fighting in the freedom cause that we began. So, tonight, each of us joins in saluting the heroes of the Lomba River and their leader, the hope of Angola, Jonas Savimbi.

So, you see, like the Panama Canal in 1976, foreign policy issues like defense spending and aid to the freedom fighters may prove the sleeper issues of the year.

So, let me urge you all to return to your organizations and communities and to tell your volunteers and your contributors that the President said that they're needed now as never before, that the crucial hour is approaching, that the choice before the American people this year is of overwhelming importance:

115

whether to hand the government back to the liberals or move forward with the conservative agenda into the 1990s.

My fellow conservatives, let's get the message out loud and clear. The Washington liberals and the San Francisco Democrats aren't extinct; they're just in hiding, waiting for another try. Well, let's make it clear to the American people that they must choose this year between those who are enemies of big government and the friends of the freedom fighters and, on the other hand, those who are advocates of Federal power and a foreign policy of illusion. So, let the choice be clear. Will it be "blame America first," or will it be "On to Democracy" and "Forward for Freedom"?

And freedom is the issue. The stakes are that high. You know, recently Nancy and I saw together a moving new film, the story of Eleni. It's a true story. A woman at the end of World War II, caught in the Greek civil war, a mother who, because she smuggled her children out to safety, eventually to America, was tried, tortured, and shot by the Greek Communists.

It is also the story of her son, Nicholas Gage, who grew up to become an investigative reporter with the *New York Times* and who, when he returned to Greece, secretly vowed to take vengeance on the man who had sent his mother to her death.

But at the dramatic end of the story, Nick Gage finds he cannot extract the vengeance he has promised himself. To do so, Mr. Gage writes, would have relieved the pain that had filled him for so many years, but it would also have broken the one bridge still connecting him to his mother and the part of him most like her. As he tells it: "...her final cry, before the bullets of the firing squad tore into her, was not a curse on her killers but an invocation of what she died for, a declaration"—how that cry was echoed across the centuries, her cry was a cry of love—" 'My children!' " A cry for all the children of the world, a hope that all of them may someday live in peace and freedom.

And how many times have I heard it in the Oval Office while tryng to comfort those who have lost a son in the service of our nation and the cause of freedom. "He didn't want to die," the wife of Major Nicholson said at Fort Belvoir last year about her

116

husband, "and we didn't want to lose him, but he would gladly lay down his life again for America."

So, we owe something to them, you and I. To those who've gone before—Major Nicholson, Eleni, the heroes at the Lomba River—and to the living as well—Andrei Sakharov, Lech Walesa, Adolfo Calero, Jonas Savimbi—their hopes reside in us as ours do in them.

Some 20 years ago I told my fellow conservatives that "You and I have a rendezvous with destiny." And tonight that rendezvous is upon us. Our destiny is now. Our cause is still, as it was then, the cause of human freedom. Let us be proud that we serve together, and brave in our resolve to push on now toward that final victory so long sought by the heroes of our past and present and now so near at hand.

Thank you. God bless you.

XI

A Future That Works

The Ronald Reagan who spoke to the CPAC conference this year was an embattled President.

This address was delivered three months after the 1986
elections, during which Republicans lost control of the
Senate. Deepening the demoralization brought on by the
loss was the revelation of the Iran–Contra operation which
had the media and liberal politicians howling with indig-
nation.

The Iran–Contra affair—the major crisis of his presidency — would cost Mr. Reagan more than a year of
precious time and much-needed momentum.

The President also spoke at the outset of the bicenten-
nial of the U.S. Constitution, however, and in this address
he chose to emphasize the positive, evoking the vision of
the country's founders and their legacy bequeathed in the
Constitution.

He linked the essence of the conservative cause to that of
the Founders. "Modern conservatism is an active, not a
reactive philosophy," he said, affirming values that are at
the heart of civilization.

As conservatives, the President said, "we must offer a
vision of a future that works, a positive agenda for positive
results."

THE PRESIDENT. Thank you. Thank you very much. Thank
you.

AUDIENCE. Four more years! Four more years! Four more
years!

118

THE PRESIDENT. Thank you all. Thank you. As Henry VIII said to each one of his six wives "I won't keep you long."

Fellow conservatives and dear friends, it's such a pleasure to be with you again. I see so many who've served our cause with such distinction over the years. David Keene and so many others of you deserve accolades for commitment and dedication.

What we've accomplished these last six years wouldn't have been possible without a solid foundation, one painstakingly laid. And much of that work was done by men and women who were content to make their contribution knowing their names would never be enshrined, individuals who didn't make the clips when the recent documentary about the conservative movement was made. Two centuries ago the Americans who were the bulwark of the cause of liberty and independence— ho backed up the Hancocks, the Jeffersons, and the Patrick Henrys—were of similar stock.

And so, today let me express my appreciation to all of you. You are truly freedom's team. The going may be a little rough at this moment, but let no one doubt our resolve.

You know these last several weeks I've felt a little bit like that farmer that was driving his horse and wagon to town for some grain and had a head-on collision with a truck. And later was the litigation involving claims for his injuries, some of them permanent. And he was on the stand and a lawyer said to him, "Isn't it true that while you were lying there at the scene of the accident someone came over to you and asked you how you were feeling, and you said you never felt better in your life?" And he said, "Yes, I remember that."

Well, later he's on the stand and the witnesses were there— the lawyer for the other side is questioning—and he said, "When you gave that answer about how you felt, what were the circumstances?" "Well," he said, "I was lying there and a car came up and a deputy sheriff got out." He said, "My horse was screaming with pain—had broken two legs. The deputy took out his gun, put it in the horse's ear, and finished him off." And he said, "My dog was whining with pain—had a broken back." "And," he said, "he went over to him and put the gun in his

119

ear." "And then," he says, "he turned to me and says now, how are you feeling?"

But getting back to our resolve: six years ago we won a great victory, and we don't intend to let anyone again drag our beloved country into the murky pit of collectivism and statism.

This is the 200th anniversary of our Constitution, and no cloud will dim the shining light of our remembrance. This year we rededicate ourselves to the shared values and the common purpose that have given our nation unrivaled prosperity and freedom. We hear the cynics, but pay them no mind. We pass by the pessimists and the doomsayers knowing that they'll always be with us, but confident that they no longer can hold our country back unless we let them. We see before us a future worthy of our past and a tomorrow greater than all our yesterdays. If there's any message that I wish to convey today it is: be of good cheer. We're coming back and coming back strong.

Our confidence flows not from our skill at maneuvering through political mazes, not from our ability to make the right deal at the right time, nor from any idea of playing one interest group off against the other. Unlike our opponents, who find their glee in momentary political leverage, we garnish our strength of purpose from a commitment to ideals that we deeply believe are not only right but that work.

Ludwig Von Mises, that great economist, once noted: "People must fight for something they want to achieve, not simply reject an evil." Well, the conservative movement remains in the ascendancy because we have a bold, forward-looking agenda. No longer can it be said that conservatives are just anti-Communist. We are, and proudly so, but we are also the keepers of the flame of liberty. And as such, we believe that America should be a source of support, both moral and material, for all those on God's Earth who struggle for freedom. Our cause is their cause, whether it be in Nicaragua, Afghanistan, or Angola. When I came back from Iceland I said—and I meant it—American foreign policy is not simply focused on the prevention of war but the expansion of freedom.

Modern conservatism is an active, not a reactive philosophy. It's not just in opposition to those vices that debase character

120

and community, but affirms values that are at the heart of civilization. We favor protecting and strengthening the family, an institution that was taken for granted during the decades of liberal domination of American government.

The family, as became clear in the not-too-distant past, is taken for granted at our peril. Victimized most were the least fortunate among us, those who sorely needed the strength and protection of the family. A federal welfare system, constructed in the name of helping those in poverty, wreaked havoc on the poor family—tearing it apart, eating away at the underpinnings of their community, creating fatherless children, and unprecedented despair. The liberal welfare state has been a tragedy beyond description for so many of our fellow citizens, a crime against less fortunate Americans. The welfare system cries out for reform, and reformed it will be. And when it is, the No. 1 question that must be asked of every change is: will this strengthen the family?

Now, personally, I think that criterion should guide our decisions, not just in welfare reform, but in the deliberations of every department and agency. And if the answer is negative, the proposal should be sent to the Heritage Foundation for study, and you can bet they'll know what to do with it.

Our positive stance on family and children is consistent with our heartfelt convictions on the issue of abortion. Here again, we're not just against an evil. We're not just anti-abortion; we're pro-life. Many who consider abortion the taking of human life understandably feel frustrated and perhaps a sense of helplessness in bringing about the legal changes that we all seek. Progress has been slow and painful, and all the while the taking of unborn lives continues. Well, while we keep up the pressure for a change of law, there is something that can be done. Those of us who oppose abortion can and should aggressively move forward with a positive adoption versus abortion campaign.

We must see to it that adoption is a readily available alternative and is an encouraged course of action. I would like to commend those in our movement, while not easing up on applying political pressure, who have been involved in provid-

121

ing counseling and services, especially to unwed mothers. Every time a choice is made to save an unborn baby's life, it is reason for joy. In the meantime, we in government will see to it that not one tax dollar goes to encouraging any woman to snuff out the life of her unborn child and that eventually the life of the unborn again comes within the protection of the law.

Last week we sent to Congress legislation to enact on a permanent, government-wide basis the Hyde amendment restriction on federal funding of abortion. Our proposal would also cut off funding, under Title X, to private organizations that refer or perform abortions except when the mother's life is in danger. I hope all of you will join in the bipartisan effort to enact this much needed legislation.

Conservatives are working for a society where children are cherished and in school are taught not only reading, writing, and arithmetic but fundamental values as well. And in striving for this, we will not compromise in our commitment to restore the right to pray to the school children of America. We want a strong America, and we know the truth behind President Eisenhower's words, when he quoted a young Frenchman's observation that if America ceases to be good, America will cease to be great.

The moral underpinnings of our country must be able to bear the weight of today if we're to pass on to the next generation an America worth having. And again, we're positive, and our eyes are on the future. And that's why so many of today's young people are supporting our cause. And believe me, as I was running for re-election, I saw them at every stop—those young people—full of life, enjoying their freedom, and enthusiastic about the United States of America. I have to tell you, you young people are a new experience for us. We went through some years when you weren't cheering us and it's wonderful to have you on our side. Well, our greatest political challenge is to find the formula that will mobilize our broad support among young people. Clearly, they aren't just looking for youthful appearances. My birthday cake's beginning to look more and more like a bonfire every year!

We must offer a vision of a future that works, a positive

agenda for positive results. And we must not be so much against big government and high taxes as we are in favor of higher take-home pay and more freedom. And we've proven it works. With an emphasis on enterprise, investment, and work, on jobs and opportunity, we turned around economic decline and national malaise and set in motion one of the longest periods of peacetime economic growth and job creation in postwar history.

The pundits, you know, the pundits told us that we couldn't expect to get anything accomplished, even before we got to Washington. Now, they're trying to bring the curtain down before the show is over. Well, I learned a lesson in my former profession. So, let me give you a tip: we're saving the best stuff for the last act.

Thank you. Thank you very much. Thank you.

AUDIENCE: Four more years! Four more years! Four more years!

THE PRESIDENT: Thank you very much. Our game plan is still the best one in town. The notion that government controls, central planning, and bureaucracy can provide cost-free prosperity has now come and gone the way of the hula-hoop, the Nehru jackets, and the all-asparagus diet. Throughout the world the failure of socialism is evident.

There's an underground joke that's told in the Soviet Union, for example, about a teacher who asked one of the young students, Ivan, what life is like in the United States. And dutifully Ivan said, "Half the people are unemployed and millions are hungry or starving." "Well, then," the teacher asks, "then what is the goal of the Soviet Union?" Ivan said, "to catch up with the United States."

Seriously though, today free enterprise is propelling us into a new technological era. Small businesses throughout our land now have computer capability, which a decade ago was available only to large corporations. The economic vitality pushing our country into the 21st Century is broad-based and irreversible — and it's not coming from the top, but from the bottom. The creative talents of our citizenry, always America's greatest asset, are being magnified by state-of-the-art technology and

123

put to work for our benefit as never before. We have every reason to be optimistic.

Our scientific advances offer us new methods of meeting the challenges we face as a people. One of the first significant questions to emerge as a result of our rapid progress deals with the Strategic Defense Initiative. I see you know that that is our effort to develop a way of protecting mankind from the threat of ballistic missiles. It holds the promise of someday making those missiles, deadly weapons that have been the cause of such dread, obsolete.

We have offered to share the benefits of our SDI program with the Soviet Union, perhaps as part of an overall agreement to dramatically reduce our respective nuclear arsenals. But let me make this clear: a defense against ballistic missiles is just one of many new achievements that will be made possible by the incredible technological progress that we are enjoying.

Each step forward improves our lives, adding to our ability to produce and build and generate wealth. Yet each step also has strategic implications. SDI, as I say, is one. Let there be no doubt, we have no intention of being held back because our adversary cannot keep up. We will use our scientific skills to make this a more prosperous world and to enhance the security of our own country. We must not and will not bargain our future away.

Six years ago we came to Washington at a time of great national uncertainty. The vigor and confidence so evident in our land today reflect more than luck. They are the outgrowth of ideas that stress freedom for the individual and respect for the humane and decent values of family, God and neighborhood.

We are giving our children the greatest gift that is within our power to give, the one we received from those who came before us: a strong, free, and opportunity-filled America. And I thank you for all that you have done and continue to do to make certain that we do just that.

And so, thank you, and God bless you all.

XII

On the Frontier of Freedom
FEBRUARY 11, 1988

Ronald Reagan's last CPAC speech as President gave the *apologia* for his seven year stewardship that one would expect from a president nearing the end of his term.

The economic record of his administration is covered in some detail, juxtaposing the success of the Reagan years with the failures of the Carter administration. The President also commented with great pride about his success in reshaping the federal judiciary by nominating to the bench judges who were strict constructionists.

On the foreign policy front, the President defended his INF treaty with the Soviets (a treaty that had divided conservatives) and, remarking the narrow defeat of his request for military aid to the Nicaraguan Contras, he pledged to continue the push to aid the freedom fighters.

Speaking just before the New Hampshire GOP presidential primary, Mr. Reagan refused to endorse a candidate for the GOP nomination. He pledged instead to work hard for whomever won, and exhorted his conservative listeners to do likewise.

Looking to the future, he urged his "troops" to carry on the fight. They were, and would remain, soldiers on "the frontier of freedom."

THANK YOU VERY MUCH. It's great to be here tonight, and I'm delighted to see so many old friends. And now let's get right to it. First, there's the INF treaty. How do you think I felt when Gorbachev called a week and a half ago and asked me if our first group of on-site inspectors could be the Denver Broncos' pass defense? (Laughter.) And then along came the House vote on Contra aid—I felt so terrible, I nearly called Dan Reeves and John Elway to tell them what a rough week I'd had.

But seriously, while the Denver Broncos are all terrific athletes and people, each one of us has to congratulate the Washington Redskins. Believe me, the House action on the Contra vote was a missed chance at a victory for peace in Central America. It's great to know there are some people in Washington who play to win. And believe me, I'll be getting back to that topic in a few minutes.

By the way, something odd happened just before I got here tonight that I think you should know about. I got a message from Dave Keane reminding me that this was the eve of Lincoln's birthday—and suggesting I go upstairs and check on the ghost in Lincoln's bedroom. I did. And what do you know, there was Stan Evans dressed as Abe Lincoln. And he kept saying, "Listen to Jesse Helms."

Actually, I do want to thank you for that warm welcome, but I hope tonight isn't going to be like what happened to that fellow I knew back in Hollywood in those movie days—and, oh, how I hope I have't told you this one before.

We had an actor that was in Hollywood, and he was only there long enough to get enough money to go to Italy, because he aspired to an operatic career. And then after some time there, in Milan, Italy, where he was studying, he was invited to sing at La Scala—the very spiritual fountainhead of opera. They were doing *Pagliacci*, and he sang the beautiful aria, *Vesti La Giuba*. And he received such thunderous and sustained applause from the balconies and the orchestra seats that he had to repeat the aria as an encore. And again the same sustained, thunderous applause. And again he sang *Vesti La Giuba*. And this went on until finally he motioned for quiet, and he tried to tell them how full his heart was at that reception—his first time out. But he said, "I have sung *Vesti La Giuba* nine times now. My voice is gone. I cannot do it again." And a voice from the balcony said, "You'll do it 'till you get it right." Well, let's get it right tonight. And let's start where we should start.

A couple of weeks ago, I talked about the state of our Union, and tonight I'd like to talk about something that I think in many ways is synonymous: the state of our movement. During the past year, plenty of questions have been asked about the conservative movement by some people who were surprised to find out back in 1980 that there was such a thing. I mean a powerful new political movement capable of running a victorious national campaign based on an unabashed appeal to the American people for conservative ideas and principles.

Well, we conservatives have been in Washington now for a while and we occasionally need to remind ourselves what brought us here in the first place: our unshakable, root-deep, all-encompassing skepticism about the capital city's answer to the UFO, that bizarre, ever-tottering but ever-flickering saucer in the sky called "The Prevailing Washington Wisdom."

And, right now, some of the Potomac seers are saying we conservatives are tired; or they're saying we don't have a candidate, some of those candidates in the other party saying how easy it's going to be to win the presidency for their liberal agenda because they can run on, of all things, this administration's economic record. Boy, have I got news for them. They're seeing flying saucers again. I've even got a quote for them. It's from Napoleon—the morning of Waterloo—at breakfast with his generals. This is true. He said, "I tell you what—Wellington is a bad general. The English are bad trips. We'll settle the matter by lunchtime."

Well, my fellow conservatives, I think that's exactly what this year is about—settling the matter by lunchtime. Letting the liberals in Washington discover once again the lesson they refuse to learn. Letting them know just how big our election year will be because of booming economic growth and individual opportunity; and how big an election year ball and chain they've given themselves with a seven-year record of opposition to the real record. But, most of all, letting them know that the real friends of the conservative movement aren't those entrenched in the capital city for 50 years; the real friends of the conservative movement are an entity that gets heard from in a big way every four years and who, I promise you, are going to be

127

heard from this year. I'm talking about those who, if the case is aggressively put before them, will vote for limited government, family values, and a tough, strong foreign policy every single time. I'm talking about those believers in common sense and sound values, your friends and mine, the American people.

You see, those who underestimate the conservative movement are the same people who always underestimate the American people. Take the latest instance. As I mentioned, in recent months some people—and I'm not mentioning any names because I don't want to build up any candidacies before New Hampshire but you know who they are—have actually taken it upon themselves to prove to the American people that they've been worse off under this administration than they were back in the Carter years of the '70s.

Now I agree with you, this takes some doing. How do they manage it? Well, you see, any statistical comparison of the two recent administrations would start with 1977 to 1981 as the budget years of the last administration, and 1981 to 1987 as the pertinent years for this one. Now, that sounds reasonable enough. But our opponents have a new approach, one that would have embarrassed even the emperor's tailors. They take the years 1977, to up to 1983—and then they stop. So you see, not only do 1984 and 1985 not get counted in their data base, but they include in this administration's economic record four years of the last Democratic administration. As columnist Warren Brookes pointed out in an article published in the *Washington Times*, "all of the foreshortened Reagan gains are nullified by the Carter losses, so they look like no gains at all, or, worse, losses." Our successes, in short, are buried under the last administration's failures.

But the truth is otherwise. Because under the last administration real per capita disposable income rose at only one percent annual rate, only half the two percent rate of increase under this administration—a gain that has totaled 12.4 percent in six years. Under the last administration, median family income declined 6.8 percent while under this administration it went up 9.1 percent. Or take the real after-tax labor income per hour. If you use the approach adopted by our liberal critics, you see a 4.5

128

percent decline. But the truth is that that figure fell 8.5 percent under the last administration and we turned this around and accounted for an 8.9 percent increase.

Under the last administration, the average weekly wage went down an incredible 10 percent in real terms, which accounted for the worst drop in postwar history. Here again, we've stopped the decline. And that's not to mention what all this has meant in terms of opportunity for women, for blacks, and minorities, the very groups our opponents say they most want to help.

Well, since the recovery began, 70 percent of the new jobs have been translated into opportunities for women; and black and other minority employment has risen twice as fast as all other groups. Minority family income has also increased at a rate over 40 percent faster than other groups. In addition, since 1983, 2.9 million people have climbed out of poverty, and the poverty rate has declined at the fastest rate in more than 10 years.

So, think for a moment on what these statistics mean and the kind of political nerve and desperation it takes to try to sell the American people on the idea that in the 1980s they never had it so bad. The truth is, we're in the 63rd month of this non-stop expansion. Real Gross National Product growth for 1987 was 3.8 percent, defying the pessimists and even exceeding our own forecast—which was criticized as being too rosy at the time—by more than one half percent. Inflation is down from 13.5 per cent in 1980 to only around 4 percent or less this year. And there's over 15 million new jobs.

So, believe me, I welcome this approach by the opposition. And I promise you, every time they use it, I'll just tell the story of a friend of mine who was asked to a costume ball a short time ago—he slapped some egg on his face and went as a liberal economist.

Now the reason I spell out these statistics and stress this economic issue should be very clear. You know that some cynics like to say that the people vote their pocketbook. But that's not quite the point. Economic issues are important to the people not simply for reasons of self-interest. They know the whole body politic depends on economic stability; the great crises have come for democracies when taxes and inflation ran out of control and undermined social relations and basic institutions. The American people know what limited government, tax cuts, deregulation, and the move towards privatization have meant. It's meant the largest peacetime expansion in our history, and I can guarantee you they won't want to throw that away for a return to budgets beholden to the liberal special interests.

No, I think the economic record of conservatives in power is going to speak for itself. But now let's turn to another area. For two decades we've been talking about getting justices on the Supreme Court who cared less about criminals and more about the victims of crime, justices who knew that the words "original intent" referred to something more than New Year's resolutions and fad diets. And then, seven months ago a seat opened on the Supreme Court. And even before our first nominee was announced, a campaign was planned unlike any that has ever been waged for or against a judicial nominee in the history of our country. And let me acknowledge once again my admiration for one of the courageous defenders, not only in our time but in all time, of the principles of our Constitution, yes, of its original intent—Judge Robert Bork.

One of America's most cherished principles—the independence and integrity of our judiciary—was under siege. And the American people, who have always been with the ultimate guarantors of the Constitution, began to say with clarity and finality, it must never happen again. So when I nominated a judge who could as easily have been my first nominee, there was hardly a peep of protest. And Judge Kennedy is now going to be Justice Kennedy. And since our opponents won't, I'll let you in on a secret—Judge Kennedy will be just the kind of justice that you and I've been determined to put on the Court. Anyway, any man who teaches law school in a tri-corner hat and a powdered wig is okay by me on original intent.

Let's look at how far and how successfully we've carried the battle into the lower courts. Just look at the statistics on criminal sentencing. In few places can you see more clearly the collapse of the liberal stranglehold on our courts. The most recent statistics show federal judges imposed prison sentences that

130

averaged 32 percent longer than those handed down during 1979. Robbery sentences were 10 percent longer; drug offenses 38 percent longer; and weapons offenses 41 percent longer.

The great legal debates of the past two decades over criminal justice have, at their root, been debates over a strict versus expansive construction of the Constitution. The Constitution, as originally intended by the framers, is itself tough on crime, and protective of the victims of crime. For so long the liberal message to our national culture was tune in, turn on, let it all hang out. And now they see conservatives taking the lead as our nation says "no" to drugs, and "yes" to family, and "absolutely" to schools that teach basic skills, basic values, and basic discipline. And it's no wonder that our nation admires a man who believes in teaching values in education, and talks turkey to teachers, parents, and educators such as our Secretary of Education, Bill Bennett.

And so I say to you tonight that the vision and record that we will take aggressively to the American people this November is a vision that all Americans, except a few on the left, share. A vision of a nation that believes in the heroism of ordinary people living ordinary lives; of tough courts and safe streets, of a drug-free America where schools teach honesty, respect, love of learning and, yes, love of country; a vision of a land where families can grow in love and safety and where dreams are made with opportunity. This is the vision; this is the record; this is the agenda for victory this year.

Well, that's the record then on the economy and the social issues. Now, let's turn to foreign policy.

I want to be clear tonight about the vote on Contra aid. It was a setback to the national security interests of the United States, and a sad moment for the cause of peace and freedom in Central America. Until now the carrot-and-stick approach has worked in forcing a communist regime to relax some of its repression. But now, the action by the House of Representatives removes one part of that formula and goes only with the carrot. The effect of this vote then was to thrust the promises of democracy of the Sandinista communists—the kind of promises that no communist regime in history has ever carried out, and that this regime was likely to carry out only under continued pressure. The effect of this vote was to rest the hopes for peace and democracy in Central America purely and simply on the word of the communist regime in Managua. This course is, and I repeat, a risk to America's national security.

But you know, I read something the other day and it's worth a note here. One of those opposing aid to the freedom fighters said it was important to get a 20-vote margin. Well, as you know, it was nothing like that—if we could have turned around four or five votes, we would have won. Last week's vote was not the final word, only a pause. Last week, the bad news was the lost vote in the House. But the good news was our support in the Senate and the overwhelming number of House Republicans who voted with us and those 47 Democrats who braved the threats of reprisals to vote for Contra aid.

So, let me make this pledge to you tonight: we're not giving up on those who are fighting for their freedom—and they aren't giving up either. I'll have more to say on this in a few weeks. For now, I'll leave it at this: get ready—the curtain hasn't fallen, the drama continues.

While we're on foreign policy, let me turn for just a moment to what I said in that December interview while Mr. Gorbachev was here. You know, Ben Wattenberg was one of the journalists there, and he brought up a speech I made back in 1982 to the British Parliament. And he asked me if what I really was saying was what I said in England: that if the West remained resolute, the Soviets would have to, at some point, deal with their own internal problems and crises, that the tides of history are shifting in favor of the cause of freedom. Well, I believed then, and I believe now, that we must consider what we're seeing—or the steps in that direction. This hardly means accepting the Soviets at face value. Few of us can forget what that has led to in the past. FDR was quoted as saying during his dealings with Stalin —with the Soviets in '44: "Stalin doesn't want anything but security for his country and I think that if I give him everything I possibly can and ask nothing from him in return, noblesse oblige, he won't try to annex anything and will work with me for a world democracy and peace."

Well, no, there is no room for illusion. Our guard is up, our watch is careful. We shall not be led by—or misled by atmospherics. We came to Washington with a common-sense message that the world is a dangerous place where the only sure route to peace and the protection of freedom is through American strength. In no place has this thesis of peace through strength been tested more than on the matter of intermediate-range nuclear forces (INF). In deploying over 400 SS–20s, with over 1,200 warheads, against our friends and allies in Europe and Asia over the past decade, the Soviets were playing a high-stakes game of geopolitical blackjack. The prize was Europe—the strategy, discredit America's deterrence and undermine the NATO alliance. But we and our allies turned over a winning hand, deploying in Europe Pershing II and ground-launched cruise missiles that provided an effective counter to the new Soviet missiles, and Moscow finally stopped upping the stakes.

What I would like to see is for some of those who've been praising our INF treaty to show they've learned its true lesson and vote to maintain an adequate defense budget, our work on a strategic defense against ballistic missiles, and, yes, aid to the freedom fighters in Nicaragua.

And while we're on the subject of our nation's defense—you know, there's a man I want to talk about tonight who said once that "the definition of happiness was service to a noble cause." No one has done that better, and tonight I salute Cap Weinberger for all he's done for America.

But at the same time we must not look at any single step alone —we must see not just the INF treaty but also the advance of SDI and, most important, the growing democratic revolution around the globe against totalitarian regimes. We should engage the Soviets in negotiations to deter war and keep the peace. But at the same time, we must make clear our own position, as I have throughout these negotiations. In sitting down to these negotiations, we accept no moral equivalency between the cause of freedom and the rule of totalitarianism.

And we understand that the most important change of all is this: that containment is no longer enough, that we no longer can be satisfied with an endless stalemate between liberty and repression. That arms reduction negotiations, development and testing of SDI, and our help for freedom fighters around the globe must express the clear goal of American foreign policy. To deter war, yes. To further world peace, yes. But, most of all, to advance and protect the cause of world freedom so that some day every man, woman, and child on this Earth has as a birthright the full blessings of liberty.

We've seen dramatic change in these seven years. Who would have guessed seven years ago that we would see tax rates drop from 70 percent to 28 percent, the longest peacetime economic boom in our history, or a massive shift in world opinion toward the ideas of free enterprise and political freedom?

I know some of you are impatient with the pace of this change. But if I might repeat a story I told when I addressed you for the first time as President—I had the pleasure in appearing before a Senate committee once while I was still Governor. And I was challenged there because there was a Republican president in the White House at the time, who'd been there for some time—and why hadn't we corrected everything that had gone wrong. And the only way I could think to answer him is, I told him about a ranch many years ago that Nancy and I acquired. It had a barn with eight stalls in it, in which they kept cattle— cows. We wanted to keep horses. Well, the accumulation within the stalls had built up the floor to the place that it wasn't even tall enough for horses in there. And so there I was, day after day, with a pick and shovel, lowering the level of those stalls, which had accumulated over the years. And I told this senator who'd asked that question that I discovered that you didn't undo in a relatively short time what it had taken some 15 years to accumulate.

We have not only been undoing the damage of the past; we've put this nation on the upward road again. And, in the process, the differences between the liberals and conservatives have become clear to the American people. We want to keep taxes low, they want to raise them; we send in budgets with spending cuts and they want to ignore them; we want the balanced budget amendment and the line-item veto and they oppose them; we want tough judges and tough anti-crime legislation, they hold them both up in the Congress.

You'd be surprised how many judges are waiting out there before they—so that they have to pass on them before they can take their office, and they've been waiting for months. We want a prayer amendment, they won't let it come to a vote in the House; we stress firmness with the Soviets, they try to pass legislation that would tie our hands in arms negotiations and endanger our defenses. But I say, we have a program and a plan for the American people—a program to protect Amercian jobs by fighting the menace of protectionism, to move forward at flank speed with SDI, to call America to conscience on the issue of abortion on demand, to mention, as I did in my State of the Union Address, the overwhelming importance of family life and family values.

That's a case to take to the American people. That's a fighting agenda. I intend to campaign vigorously for whoever our nominee is, and tonight I ask each of you to join me in this important crusade. Let's ask the American people to replenish our mandate. Let's tell them if they want four more years of economic progress and the march of world freedom, they must help us this year. Help us settle the matter before lunchtime. Help make 1988 the year of the Waterloo liberal.

I just have to add here, when you look at the figures overall— that they have the nerve even to still be out there and campaigning. (*Laughter*)

We mustn't just think that electing the president is enough. We've been doing that for more than half-a-century. We have—in the 50 years between 1931 and 1980, only four years in that period was there a Republican majority in both houses of the Congress—two years in Eisenhower's regime, two years in Truman's. But for 46 of those 50 years, they controlled the Congress. Every Democratic president, except for those two years, had a Democratic Congress. Every Republican president had a Democratic Congress, except for those two years in Eisenhower's regime. And now, in the last seven years added to that—yes, for six of those years we had one House. But except for the four years, for 58 years it will be our opponents holding the House of Representatives, where so much legislation and authorization for spending and so forth comes in. And in all those 58 years, there have only been eight single years in which there was a balanced budget. So, who's at fault for the deficit today?

Back when the great society—when the war on poverty began, which poverty won—from 1965 to 1980—in those 15 years, the federal budget increased to five times what it had been in '65. And the deficit increased to 38 times what it had been just 15 years before. It's built-in, it's structural. And you and I need to get representatives not only in the Executive Branch, but out there in the legislature, so that we can change that structure that is so built-in, and that threatens us with so much harm.

Well, I've gone on too long for all of you here, but I just wantedo—I couldn't resist, because you're the troops. You're out there on the frontier of freedom. One young soldier over there in Korea—one of our men—saluted me when I visited there, and very proudly said, "Mr. President, we're on the frontier of freedom." Well, so are you.

Thank you. God bless you all.